Taking Responsibility Taking Direction
WHITE ANTI-RACISM IN CANADA

Sheila Wilmot

ARBEITER RING PUBLISHING • WINNIPEG

Printed in Canada by the workers at Houghton Boston.
Cover image and design: Mike Carroll   Layout: Tim Scarth

With assistance of the Manitoba Arts Council/Conseil des Arts du Manitoba.
We acknowledge the support of the Canada Council for the Arts for our publishing
program.

Library and Archives Canada Cataloguing in Publication
Wilmot, Sheila Jane, 1963–
Taking responsibility, taking direction : white anti-racism
in Canada / Sheila Jane Wilmot.
ISBN 1-894037-24-3
1. Racism—Canada. 2. Canada—Race relations. 3. Whites—
Canada—Political activity. 4. Race discrimination—Canada. I. Title.
FC104.W59 2005   305.8'00971   C2005-906753-5

Contents

Acknowledgements

There are a number of people who kindly took the time to do talk with me about their experiences or give me access to their materials. For this I would like to thank Sarita Ahooja, Julia Barnett, Neil Braganza, Dave Brophy, Emily Chan, Mary Gellatly, Raghu Krishnan, Deena Ladd, Mary-Jo Nadeau, Zainab Taiyeb and Carol Wall. Others were good enough to take the time to read early versions of the manuscript for this book. The diverse perspectives and insights of Leela Acharya, Farshid Baghai, Katayoun Baghai, Joanne Knutson, Sonia Singh and Hamid Sodeifi were invaluable. In particular, I cannot thank Susan Bender and David Camfield enough, both of whom not only read various drafts but who also were firmly in my corner, personally and politically, throughout the whole process. The support of the Toronto Women's Bookstore, through accepting my course proposal based on this book's material, has been instrumental for initiating the process of engaging the local community with the book's ideas. Many thanks to Arbeiter Ring in general, for taking this project on, and also to Pat Sanders in particular for her patient and detailed copy editing. And, finally, thanks to Mike Johnson for his support and encouragement in figuring out one of the hardest jobs of all, finishing.

Why White Anti-Racism?

The Canadian Stage For Anti-Racism

In June 1993 there were multiple, vicious, "unprovoked and racially motivated" attacks on Sri Lankan Tamil men in downtown Toronto. One man, Gunalan Muthulingam, was beaten so severely that he died three days later. The community response to this was immediate and broad: South Asian, Latino, Black, Filipino and Korean individuals and groups stepped forward, as did lesbian and gay, pro-choice, anti-poverty and feminist organizations and people. In the months following a large June 28 demonstration, they and others founded the Toronto Coalition Against Racism (TCAR), whose aim it was "to build a broad, mass action coalition to fight racism wherever it manifests itself."[1]

TCAR was truly a multiracial and sectoral coalition, with an anti-oppression analysis that also challenged the structure of capitalism as a core reason for the perpetuation of racism. Not only organizing in defense of the Tamil community, TCAR campaigns also included the fight against the federal imposition of an additional sponsorship application fee (the $975 "head tax"), the local harassment and federal policy attacks on the Somali community, the police violence against people of colour and/or poor people, and putting racism on the agenda before and after election campaigns. There were press conferences, community meetings, multilingual poster campaigns and vibrant demonstrations. Although many people involved in the movement would readily admit their project was challenging, their commitment, determination and impact were strong.[2] One early TCAR member remembers an early demo as having had

> thousands of people there, on a nice summer afternoon, from a number of communities but particularly from the Sri Lankan/Tamil community. What really stood out for me was the fact that it really came out of the community. It started and marched through their neighbourhood (not in front of the cop shop or government building), it was full of people of colour (80% or more).[3]

TCAR has not been around for many years now and their coalition has not yet evolved to take the next steps forward. This is both a reflection of the difficult broad social conditions we face in Canada in trying to fight street- and state-level racist attacks that have not abated in their intensity, and of the ongoing fragmented state of the left. There is much determination, many communities who still resist the day-to-day marginalization, and we see many inspiring and meaningful organizing moments; what we are lacking right now are movements.

I remember an exhilarating moment I had in the summer of 2003 while working with Justicia for Migrant Workers. Every year, about 20,000 farm workers from Mexico and the Caribbean spend up to ten months of the year in Canada, doing the lowest paid, most hazardous work in various areas of the agricultural industry. About 90% of these workers come to southern Ontario. One Sunday in September, a group of us headed out to the town of Leamington, where we knew there would be a Mexican Independence Day celebration near a local church. When we arrived, dozens of workers were already there, hanging out and chatting in small groups. One of our group members had brought copies of the tripartite agreement under which the migrants are allowed to work in Canada. The agreement is between the Canadian government, the worker's country of origin, and, formally, the worker.

With both Spanish and English copies of the agreement in hand, we mingled in the crowd. It was casual, because both Mexican consulate representatives and employers were there. We talked with a number of workers, who became quite interested in seeing a Spanish copy of the contract, which many of them had never heard of or had seen only in English. What progressed were serious, open conversations about the contradictions between their conditions, their rudimentary legal rights and how their precarious status made it extremely difficult to use the latter to improve the former. These were conversations of equals: equal in terms of our humanity but not, by a long shot, in terms of our conditions. It was a moment of possibility, of mutual respect, of traversing gender, race and class in order to connect. The moment was important for me and for many of the workers.

The thing is, though, while moments are what drive many activists on in times of low levels of struggle, a series of moments do not necessarily lead to movements. And, with a specific focus on white anti-racism, this is precisely what this book seeks to explore: while valuing the self-activity of people, the dignity of struggling in the face of incredibly difficult conditions and the humanity of our own solidarity with such struggles, we also need to take a hard, honest look at the effectiveness of what we are doing, and why it often is not.

Historically, it's generally safe to say that "there's drudgery in social change and glory for the few."[4] Yet, these days are certainly a hard time to be a social movement or union activist in Canada. That is why I wrote this book. After being a community activist for more than a decade and a half, I needed to explore the complexities of where our movements have gone and what makes it so hard to rekindle them, particularly now and specifically in the context of white anti-racism. This book is for those of us opposed to racism who want to explore its historical roots in a way that looks at social processes as a whole: how systems and people interact and evolve together over time to bring us to where we are today. This is a book of both critique and strategy, coming out of my experience in international solidarity, anti-racist, feminist and workers' rights organizing, and all that I have learned in these settings, working with an array of inspiring and driven people. What is in these pages offers a challenge to us all: the issues are complex and there is no one organizing formula to which we can just add determination and mix up a solution.

There have been other, likely even harder, times too in history. But our lives are happening in this period now, so, rather than despair, we can actively grapple with how to deal with today's world, in order to see future possibilities for change. Many people are working hard in various corners of Canada: some are fighting in already precarious work conditions to get the millions of dollars in back wages owed by employers; others are struggling against the rising tide of anti-immigrant laws and actions; and many unionists continue to work against the erosion of their collective agreements. Periodically, there are some hopeful organizing efforts, particularly coming out of immigrant and refugee communities, but it is difficult to see the possibility in the near future for a strong, united project to change our world. There are multiple and complex reasons for the persisting low ebb of organizing for social change in Canada; one reason is the ongoing failure of white activists and unionists to really understand and collectively act against white supremacy and racism.

A large part of our context for anti-racist organizing is now one of fiercely systemic, anti-Middle Eastern racism, from new "security" laws to increased repression of immigrants and refugees. In our organizing efforts, the racism itself is not our only challenge: we also have to deal with our society's collective response to these and other neo-liberal attacks in a context in which we continue to accept the dominant idea that electoral politics is the only way democracy can function, at the same time as we are disillusioned by it. So, we "the people" get to choose one pro-capitalist party or another and, like it or not, "we" get what "we" voted for. In Canada, this is compounded by the ruling class strategy of constant federal, provincial and municipal intergovernmental public bickering and buck-passing, each creating themselves as the most socially concerned, fiscally sensible player while blaming the other for not looking after Canadians well enough.

While this implicit acceptance of being ruled changes over time and looks different in various parts of the world, on the whole, big-business owners, high-level financial managers, members of parliament, economists, politicians and newspaper owners continue to set the agenda for the "way things are" for the rest of us. While the political South has been ravaged by various forms of genocide and the siphoning of natural and financial resources for centuries, including the structural adjustment programs (SAPs) of the last few decades, the North's lesser form of SAPs hit us in the 1980s as part of the elites' response to the economic crises that started in the 1970s. This has meant the gutting of social programs, the scrapping of trade "barriers" such as cross-border import and export taxes, and plunging big-business tax rates. As Employment Insurance, welfare, day care, health care, English/French as a Second Language programs, and non-profit housing have, bit by bit, been made inaccessible to more and more people, bank profit margins and CEOs' incomes soar.

Canada also has an odd place in the world as an imperialist power that is still subordinated to the self-appointed global banker, decision maker, cop and executioner on this country's southern border.[5] Combined with mythical notions of the Canadian nation's politeness and peace-loving ways, ideas are created, maintained and driven home that because of our place in the world, in particular in relation to the US, we can do very little to change the direction of globalization, that we really are quite powerless to make fight-back efforts matter. This is not to say that no one is fighting back or trying to change things. Many people do actively dissent, in ways that also change with time and place, but still in small numbers and with little continuity.

We also cannot underestimate the impact on us of how highly privatized, individualized and commodified human life has become in our time. The collective problems caused by social program cuts and bloated corporate profit margins are continually defined and redefined as individual impediments. Apparently, a better resume, attitude and sheer tenacity are all we need to just get out there and "make it." From employment and other support services, to the explosion in business training "opportunities" (from career colleges to whole new wings of universities), the daily message is that change in our lives comes from doing it all on our own and in the way that suits the needs of business.

In addition to this, social movements of the 1960s, '70s and '80s have been institutionalized through achieving some of the very demands for which activists fought. These include community-based services like rape crisis centres, immigrant and refugee settlement services, women's shelters and ethnic- and geographic-community-specific multiservice agencies. These increasingly underfunded organizations have not only become sites for generally overworked, underpaid staff and volunteers to provide important community supports; they have also become the places into which many of our feminist, anti-racist, anti-heterosexist and other movements have been pulled. Today we see some excellent politicized, non-profit, social service delivery that is mostly disconnected from any political organizing that falls outside agency- or network-specific goals and frameworks.

We are also saddled with the sectarian legacy of much of the far left. There are quite a number of small groups with their own, very specific, understanding of how capitalism and imperialism are carried out and what needs to be done about this. Generally, each little group is determined that their program is the one we must sign on to and follow. A kind of sectarianism can also be seen in certain expressions of anti-oppression politics, often in the form of ideology's setting a heavy moral tone to, for example, how we must understand and respond to white privilege. Expressions of these various beliefs can be dogmatic and prescriptive, yet have little sense of what we should be doing to get where they want us all to go. Such "my way or the highway" sectarianism continues to cast a pall over many different kinds of organizing. In my experience, many people avoid coalition-based organizing because of it.

The generally low level of working-class self-organization and struggle is related to all these factors. It also has to do with the ideological crisis on the broad left. The NDP, which is still rumoured to be a party of the working people and is officially supported by many unions, seems unable to come up with a positive, left-wing alternative in this suffocating neo-liberal period, and so follows a "pro-capitalist lite" agenda.

This rough sketch of the broad social context of our struggles gives us some idea about the overall picture for the challenges of anti-racist organizing. However, while it sheds some light on the problem, it does not explain why the anti-racism understanding and practice of white leftists continues to be so lacking. We owe this failing to the combination of the very tangible privileges we enjoy, the complexity of debilitating and useless white guilt, the lack of integrated anti-racist education we seek out and/or find, and just the plain racist attitudes and behaviours we have.

As a white community activist since the mid-1980s, I have come to think of my approach to this as constantly shifting the balance between taking responsibility and taking direction. Since all white folks benefit—whether actively or passively, whether by doing something or failing to so something—from the white supremacy fundamental to the organization of the capitalist political economy on which our society is based, since we are enrolled in the club, like it or not, we all have a social responsibility to challenge that notion of supremacy, both individually and collectively, and the resulting racism.

When we do understand this "responsibility," it seems to come often with a heavy sense of moral duty, embedded in a strange, remorse-based anti-racism: we just feel so bad about it all, and about our very selves in it all. The political responsibility then often becomes highly individualized and paralyzing. Many white activists, of various generations, seem unable to get past invoking the words "white privilege" to describe the situation and their remorse.

When we do take action, given the nature of the superiority complex we are taught as part of white racism, we white activists often seem to interpret "taking responsibility" as "taking over." This is often combined with remorse so that we feel we have just got to "power through" and get the things done that we believe will fix racism. This is where other direction is necessary: to be effective, we must also seek out, follow and encourage the leadership of people of colour, particularly non-white, working-class women. As these women are the targets of the many layers of everyday, commonsense and structural racism, sexism, class exploitation and, often, other forms of oppression, developing political relationships with them is a key piece of good organizing. A political relationship is not based on superficial, short-term alliances of convenience, such as what we experience much coalition work. Nor is it based on a narrow idea of someone's social or cultural identity. We must avoid politically homogenizing all people of colour and see political differentiation among non-white people. Building political relationships is about constructing a solid basis for working towards shared political goals. This is not to say that white activists cannot take initiative in any project unless there is 50% leadership by women of colour. On the contrary, the way our society is structured by racism means we can easily find ourselves in the majority when we'd rather not be — for example, in our workplaces — so we just have to do the work where we are. It does mean that creating the conditions for and building such relationships, making visible and respecting whoever has been marginalized by oppression, should be foundational principles of our political projects. All this will often require many white unionists and community activists to rethink our strategies and tactics, and our certainty about "what is to be done."

The responsibility/direction juggling act does not follow a straight line or look the same in every situation. But it does require a good set of anti-racist politics and a willingness to go through the muck and mire of implementing them. While many of us had many years to learn how to do this and a number of sources to draw from, and while there have been pockets of success at it, we white leftists remain collectively inadequate at dealing with white supremacy and racism. Even in cities where there are many people of colour, we whites are still far too comfortable being the large majority in certain kinds of community-based organizing and union activism. When we are uncomfortable about it, we don't seem to know what to do, how/if we should talk among ourselves and non-white activists about it, or what tools to access to improve our anti-racism. And those of us who have been activists for many years have not figured out how to both teach and learn from white youth who are struggling with white supremacy and racism.

The white anti-racism that does exist is due to the activism against racism by people of colour.[6] Most recently and specifically, it has been the feminism of women of colour that has demanded white leftists' accountability and action. In white-dominated organizations, from progressive to mainstream ones, women of colour continue to struggle for respect rather than invisibility or, at best, "tolerance." Through activist work and educational experiences, and through reading women of colour writers, I have learned about anti-racism and -white supremacy. It is important to acknowledge and underline that because multiple forms of oppression and exploitation make non-white women's various forms of struggle invisible, our associated white privilege can leave us passively taking credit or profiting from what we are learning from people of colour. Exploiting this learning happens with many white folks, from writers to professors, from musicians to artists.

One example of women of colour as the source of our learning was in Toronto in the mid-1980s at an International Women's Day march. Many women were standing on the lawn at Queen's Park, but one Black woman speaker commanded attention. She was speaking about basic anti-racism for white feminists, but it was an eye-opener for me at the time. It has been listening to women of colour, time and again over the years in such demos, in political groups and in community organizations, give the basics — sometimes patiently, at times justifiably angrily — and more that pushed me to deal with my own whiteness and all that means. As unfortunate as it is that Aboriginal women and women of colour are constantly put in the position of explaining this anti-racism, if it weren't for their determination, there would likely not be those anti-racist whites there are today.

This kind of struggle with leftists for us to "get" racism is happening in a capitalist Canadian society with a history of arrogance and destruction. From day one of the "discovery" of this part of the world, white supremacy underpinned every part of the brutal dominance of First Nations people. The ruthlessness of, first, the colonizers and, later, the nation-state has taken different forms with non-white people who came as slaves, who migrated to flee slavery, who migrated as settlers and those who continue to come as refugees and immigrants. The message of building Canada as a "white man's country" was constant in the legal arena, in the elites' political institutions, in social interaction and so in the harshness of working life. This is the root of why "many people self-identified as white experience themselves as beyond history and without community."[7] Our "ethnic identity" is not needed; it is enough that we are "white."

When we look at television, movies and music, at what is taught in schools and our families, and at the messages coming from all levels of governments, we can see how we white folks are all connected with this history; we are all marinated in its ongoing development and effect. The society we live in, the lives we have now are continuous with the past that created these conditions. So, no matter how courageous the choice may be at times, we white leftists do not become immune to white supremacy and racism when we choose to be anti-racist.

This is why open dialogue on white racism and anti-racism is so critical. My part of the current conversation in this book is mainly directed at other white activists. Part of taking responsibility is for whites to talk with other whites so people of colour don't have to do all that work. If activists and unionists of colour find something of use in this effort, then all the better. We whites have to share our analyses, what we have learned and ideas for better anti-racist action, not just with each other but in our work with non-white organizers, in order for us to become better anti-racists.

There is a lot to wade through when we try to do this. We are often bogged down in paralyzing and patronizing feelings and behaviours, including both a "fascination and guilt" with our privileged position, as well as shame and despair.[8] Arising from all this is generally a stubborn resistance to self-criticism and an avoidance of the truth to prevent feeling defensive, angry or useless.[9] On one hand, even use of the word "racism" is extremely uncomfortable for many people. On the other, as part of our defense strategy, those of us in non-profit agencies or academic settings are quite good at using anti-racist language, while doing little about racism itself.[10]

As part of the defense strategy, some of the more experienced white anti-racists don't want to deal with white people: "we distrust them as we (distrust) ourselves. Many of us (have) come to hate our own whiteness as we learned the legacy of racism. Not trusting other white folks, we (feel) better in the company of people of colour. We (do) not want to come to grips with our own history."[11] Having that comfort level working with people of colour is undeniably a good thing, but by avoiding other whites means we miss opportunities for challenging them and ourselves. As well, in the process, we can be patronizing to non-white people we work with, not giving them full credit for intellectual and organizing abilities. This can be part of the "great white hope" complex, as white activists repeatedly and uncritically seek and then maintain leadership roles in activist groups, union locals and political organizations. We are not good at taking direction from non-white people; it seems we think we know what's best, how to fix things. White supremacy has taught even most of us working-class whites that we are more competent, that we know what needs to be done. As part of this, we patronize poor people by romanticizing them, seeing them "as pillars of moral fortitude by virtue of their struggles with poverty, racism or both."[12] Romanticization and demonization can then become flip sides of the same coin: when the people of colour we have romanticized disappoint us politically, we have held them to a higher standard than we hold ourselves.

In some left circles, this part of the analysis of white racism is seen as "psychoanalysis," rather than part of looking at the political problem. What organizers often want is to move directly to more strategies to challenge racism in the system, or to finding tips on doing a better anti-racist workshop. And this is often a key problem with activism: thinking that somehow the complicated mire inside ourselves is separate from the expression of our politics. But those tangled feelings and thoughts are what inform our ideas and action. They are political, and until we are willing to grapple with their nature and where they come from, it will be difficult to be more effective anti-racists. This is not to promote soul-searching as the recipe for white anti-racist action. On the contrary: it is to improve our understanding and analysis to make our activism better. There is no way around it but through it.

The interaction of racist ideas and imagery with the various social processes through which racism has been created, through which it still lives and breathes systemically, has brought about and deepened a status quo of not only power and privilege of white folks, but also the associated fear of, disdain for and ignorance about non-white people. So there are many fronts for the anti-racist consciousness raising and action required: for example, bringing down racist immigration laws; challenging everyday acts of racist behaviour in the community and workplace; supporting the development of women of colour leadership in our political groups; pushing other whites on the "race relations approach" that apparently wishes to end racism by merely sharing what have often become frozen-in-time cultural and ethnic differences so that we find points of difference or connection superficially through embracing our appreciation of "saris, samosas and steel-bands" while avoiding what is really needed — "the "three Rs" — resistance, rebellion and rejection."[13] And while knowing and understanding each other's differences ought to be a basic starting point for human interaction, difference has gotten so exalted and mystified as to appear to be the source of our needing to improve "interracial understanding." Yet, it is not the existence of differences themselves that is the source of racism; it is economic, political and social power that has been built on the historical selection of certain attributes (for example, skin colour) for very political reasons that underpins racism. Having an historical understanding of our white supremacy and racism today is critical to knowing this.

The specific focus of this effort on white racism comes from an understanding that white supremacy has created and continues to maintain the conditions for racism and, at this point in history, vice versa. I emphasize the term "white racism," rather than simply "racism," for a reason: given the centuries of this form of oppression and how it's been used for and then reinforced by migration laws and labour and capital needs, there are often racialized hostilities among individual people and/or communities of colour. These can be understood as coming from a number of sources, including internalized racism, the variation of skin-colour-based oppression and oppression with the darkness or lightness of skin (sometimes called "lightism") among non-white people, and the impact of class location on putting certain communities of colour in less disadvantaged positions than other communities in particular places and times. One sharp example of how this can play out was in Los Angeles after the 1992 uprising.[14] There were bitter divisions between some parts of Korean- and African-American communities that had much to do with the state's historical packaging of the more middle-class East Asian communities as being more "respectable," which also resulted from laws that allow middle- and upper-class migrants privileged access to immigration. While that dynamic is often called racism — and perhaps legitimately so if one community has the social, political and/or economic power to oppress another — it is a function of the larger problem of white supremacy that privileges white-skinned people in a way different from and more far-reaching than the above dynamic. As such, whites have a particular need and responsibility to deal with white racism. When it comes to racism, that should be our main task.

Similarly, I do not take up the relationship between anti-Semitism and racism. This book is an intervention on the topic of white anti-racism, in a specific place and time: that is, here in Canada in the early years of the twenty-first century. To develop a better understanding of the topic, many avenues might be pursued for our historical reflection. Anti-Semitism could arguably be one, given that its brutal legacy is significant to understanding Zionism, on the one hand, and the social reality of Jews around the world, on the other. However, in Canada today, Jewish people of European origin have a relationship to racism that is much closer to that of white non-Jews than to that of people of colour. The lack of treatment in this book to the persecution and marginalization of Jewish people does not mean that anti-Semitism is historically disconnected from or less important than white racism. It does mean, though, that, if they were not before, racism and anti-Semitism have become somewhat different social phenomena in our place and time. That is, anti-Semitic actions and attitudes still exist but systemic anti-Semitism no longer does here in Canada.

Racism has both a complex rigidity and an historical specificity that depend on its interrelationship with class exploitation, sexism and heterosexism, and various other forms of oppression, and how these get played out in particular settings, in specific time periods.[15] Looking at how racism developed before and with capitalism, and how this happens on the ground right here and now, is looking at the problem from an integrated, historical perspective. The powers that be, the ruling class or political and business elite that run this country at all levels, tend to be decidedly ahistoric, erasing or freezing in time non-white peoples' lives, realities and resistance in the process. There is an associated determination in the dominant society to essentialize non-white people as belonging to a narrowly defined, tradition-bound cultural or religious heritage. For examples, all Iranians (both in Iran and in Canada) are seen as Muslim; South Asian women are portrayed as victims of a form of controlling and brutal sexism apparently unknown to white women; and, in general, all non-white communities are seen as homogenous without any class differences within them. In the Canadian nation-state of the last few decades, we largely have had to thank for the entrenchment of this the invention and application of multiculturalism policy and practice. White people as individuals also participate in creating and maintaining this process of erasing and freezing.

Following is an analytical framework on which this book draws. The framework attempts to integrate social processes involving racism and anti-racism in three ways: in the relationship between everyday and structural forms of white racism; in terms of the various power relations and how we experience them, particularly racism, sexism and class-exploitation; and with respect to how these power relations function and are reproduced within the historical context of imperialism and capitalism.

White anti-racism is a long, hard, lifelong road. But doing good work and being okay with ourselves "does not have to mean distancing (ourselves) from the oppressor role; it can come instead from taking a proud part in the struggle to end oppression."[16] We can work together, supporting the development of multiracial projects and organizations, by figuring out how to use white privilege to undermine the system, rather than feel remorse about its existence or ourselves. Our rage can be put to good use.

2

What I Mean When I Say ...

We use various political terms every day, often with very different ideas about what we mean. Although there are many others, I have selected the following terms because I think they are the ones used frequently by activists without a clear, common understanding of what they mean. Yet, by defining terms, I am not trying to say this is the end of the story or the only one; I am just trying to have a clear starting point from which to combine the parts — such as racism and class exploitation — into a coherent whole. To this end, I use detailed examples to bring the definitions to life.

While I do not walk through definitions of sexism and heterosexism, this will come out in the rest of the book as we see how most non-white women struggle with and resist multiple forms of oppression and class-exploitation simultaneously.

White Supremacy

The term "white supremacy" usually describes the attitudes of far-right groups, setting them and white supremacy itself apart as crazed hate groups or ideas that are aberrations in our modern society. White supremacy, however, is the backbone of the Canadian project of colonization and nation building. It is European, especially British, in origin but has not been limited to Western Europeans for many years. As the power base of those who are historically granted white-skin privilege, its ideas underpin all aspects of the dominant culture, and its social, political and economic structures. It is ultimately the source of both the ongoing brutal exclusion and subjugation of non-white people and an array of everyday and structural privileges of whites. As the backbone of the society, "conscious and unconscious ideas of white superiority and entitlement are widespread, and relations of white dominance and non-white subordination are daily reenacted across a broad array of institutions and social settings." At the least, what this means to most whites is that we are steeped in "the subjective sensation of superiority."[1] White supremacy is the ugly foundation upon which racism is built, giving us a system of often violent exclusion for non-white people and one of inclusion for whites.

Racism

With the increasingly common construction of "racism" as a hate crime, "racism has been silently transformed in the popular consciousness into acts that are abnormal, unusual and irrational,"[2] which ignores the source of these acts of racism, ignores their systemic nature. If we are disposed to recognize Canadian racism at all, the lens of hate really helps our brand of racism to maintain its so-called polite and subtle image, as racism becomes an attitudinal problem of a few backward red-necks or skinheads.

Amid the extermination and slavery, racism has an historic fluidity, with new forms being reworked and built on old ones.[3] What has been consistent is how racism is an integral part of the functioning of Canadian society. There are a number of layers of this form of oppression, but when we add together the *everyday* behaviours, acts and attitudes with *structural* laws, policies, programs and processes, we see just how *systemic* racism is. While the frequency and impact of this vary with class, they subordinate people of colour, no matter what their class.[4] The fact that immigrants of colour who are doctors and engineers are driving taxis and delivering pizzas shows one way a racist policy (the failure to accredit certain non-Canadian-trained people) can facilitate a change in class position for the worse.

Everyday racism shows itself in many ways, from ignoring people of colour in meetings to racist jokes over lunch at work, to calling non-white people "sensitive" when they call us on our racism, to acts of physical and verbal assault. It is shown, on one hand, through racist stereotypes.[5] On the other hand, "some of the humblest to the most cerebral pursuits of white people's lives are informed with racism."[6] Racism is not simply, as whites often think of it, conscious, nasty behaviour. We are implicated, even if just by our silence. There is a whole "repertoire of words, images, stories, explanations, categorizations, justifications, and rationalizations that together produce a shared understanding of the world and the status of people of colour in the world"[7] that we don't just passively receive from the media or the state. We are involved in creating them and passing them on.

This status is found too in structural racism, through immigration laws and programs that originally explicitly and now mostly implicitly give preferred access and legal status to white and middle- and upper-class migrants, making non-white working-class women the least likely to enter the country and least likely to stay for long if they do. The inhumanity of the refugee determination process is further testament to this. To meet basic needs such as housing and above poverty-wage employment, non-white people must struggle against how racism is structured into state institutions and non-governmental organizations. This can be seen in different ways. For example, a housing co-op may be largely white, not reflecting the makeup of the broader community. When challenged to implement an anti-racist outreach plan, the community may respond defensively in multiple ways, from "we're not racist; how dare you say so" to ignoring the proposal and so continuing the racist exclusion of applicants. Or, when non-white applicants are interviewed by white co-op members, a whole range of reasons may arise for not accepting people ("I don't think they'd fit in well" or "I couldn't get a read on them because they weren't good communicators"). In terms of the likelihood of getting a decently paying job, although while global capitalism continues to shrink this possibility for the whole working class, racism is structured so profoundly into the drive for profit and therefore the access to jobs that in Toronto, while 14% of European-origin (white) people are living below the poverty line, an average of 38% of non-white people live in poverty.[8] Yet, society's elites, with the complicity of most of the white working class, blame migrants and non-white people in general for economic crises — and the state spending cuts that are supposed to solve them — that are a part of capitalism's functioning.

This concrete structural and everyday reality is infused and supported by a whole range of centuries-old racist imagery that is updated to fit the times. Some ideas and images are generalized to non-white people as a whole, as in Christianity's history of seeing whiteness as good, while blackness was associated with anything negative. This kind of idea sets up white as the good, normal "us" or "self," while non-whiteness is the abnormal, feared "them" or "other." Other images that have developed in different historical circumstances of domination are directed at specific non-white people and generally are gender specific. Patricia Hill Collins details the plethora of controlling images that "offer powerful ideological justification" for the construction and maintenance of racism and sexism towards particularly Black working-class women but also Black middle-class women too.[9] From the mammy to the matriarch, the welfare mother to the middle-class Black lady, and then even to the jezebel (whore), Black women cannot turn around in society without coming up against these racist sexist ideas of who they are, what they can do and who they are allowed to be. Learning about this as whites, we can see how we participate in the continuing repression of Black women in this way. For example, it was just within the last two years that, while reading this chapter of Hill Collins's book, I realized in a sudden wave of shame that just recently I had referred to a Black woman activist I know as being "so great, so strong," while gesturing widely with my arms to expand the impression. Like Hill Collins's matriarch, the unconscious image in my mind was one-dimensional, a tough woman who can do all and keep on smiling, keep on going, no matter what. At first glance, this seems a positive image, but it not only reduces the complexity of a woman's being, it is also based on the racist stereotypes I have been steeped in since before I met her. It is distasteful to see this in ourselves, but see it and root it out we must. Even as the ruling-class use of these ideas can shift with capital's needs for working-class labour this does not happen independently of our own individual attitudes and reactions.

Taken all together, the enduring and profound level of societal organization of racism can only be called systemic. These exclusionary practices are motivated and legitimized by racism. Although bad enough in itself, racism is not just street-level name calling that can be eradicated by anti-racism workshops on March 21 every year: it is fundamental to the whole society. As a result, it becomes an integral part of the commonsense of everyday life, the unconscious idea that we all know what is good sense from our own practical experience,[10] something most white people are determined to keep invisible to ourselves even while out doing international solidarity work.

Capitalism and Class

Capitalism is a way of organizing society so that: a) competition within and dependence on the market is the basis for the making of and getting access to almost all goods and services; b) a relatively few elites make a staggering profit off this production process. In fact, capitalism's whole reason for being is profit accumulation.[11] It has existed in Canada for a few centuries and is a pervasive international phenomenon, which forms the basis for the hierarchical interaction between all countries in the world. Imperialism — the policy, practice or advocacy of extending the power of a nation, especially by taking land or by indirect control of political and economic life — is key to this international organization of capitalism.

Capitalist society is divided into classes: those who are in complete control of and benefit from exploitation and oppression (*the ruling class*); those who are not in ultimate control but do benefit and have varying degrees of control over those whose labour makes the profits (*the middle class*); and those who are doing the work that creates the profit, are unemployed generally because of the shortage of work created by how capitalism functions, or who do unpaid labour but depend on other workers' wages or paltry state social assistance payments (*the working class*).

The ruling class includes state leaders, those who run the companies that buy and sell stocks, heads of international bodies such as the International Monetary Fund (IMF) and the United Nations (UN), and owners of corporations. There is as broad a range of working-class control by middle-class management as there are middle-class incomes. For example, there are small-business people who barely break even on their bookkeeping businesses to those with fancy coffee franchises; there are professionals such as doctors and lawyers, government ministry managers, and executive directors of non-profit agencies. And the working class itself is getting more and more stratified, both in Canada and internationally, including everyone from super high-waged, unionized auto workers to the 75% of the working class that is non-unionized, a growing number of whom are making poverty wages and/or living on social assistance.

"Capitalist profits are not extracted directly from workers. The relation between (the ruling class) and labour is mediated by the market .... Profit depends on the difference between what the capitalist pays the workers and what s/he derives from the sale of the products and services supplied by the workers."[12] That is, whatever we produce and the money made from its sale belong to the boss. This can be indirect, in the case of workers in non-profit organizations. Yet, whether in the private or public sector, this relationship means that within capitalism, "there is a continuous struggle between the powerful classes and communities and those with less privilege and power."[13] Such class struggle is part of day-to-day life in capitalist society. While class itself is rooted in the workplace, class formation involves processes taking place at work, in the household and in the community.[14] As such, the impact of white supremacy, privilege and racism not only varies with time and place; it also varies with people's class position, as well as with gender.

People on both the right and the left commonly think of capitalism's classes as fixed socio-economic categories. For example, once someone crosses into the 22% tax bracket, once they own a car and/or a home of a certain value, they are often designated middle class. People are rarely located as working-class unless they are extremely low income or poor, which is not incorrect. But, what working-class people do for a living, what we produce, who profits from and controls it, our different levels of privilege within the working class and how we struggle, become invisible in this way of thinking.

Yet, the significant differential between living standards in the political North and South caused by imperialism, and the less sharp but still stark stratification within Canada, do make the understanding of class complex. The material benefits that higher waged workers have access to are connected to our understanding of what our interests are, so it is not surprising when higher wage workers see themselves as socially closer to their managers than to the person who sells them café lattes or doughnuts every morning on the way to work. And those of us on the left who make an acceptable wage typically look below us, see the privilege we have in relation to lower waged and poorer working-class folks, and so bump ourselves up to middle class. Seeing the yawning gap between our relative comfort and the struggles many people, especially in the South, have just to survive makes it difficult to think of ourselves as working class too. But to do so is not to deny class privilege; it is about really seeing where we fit in a multi-layered international system, within a multi-layered working class.

It is often the case that those who value their self-identification as middle class do not see working-class alliances until their plant closes or the state cuts funding to the community agency where they work, or they are fighting for shorter and shorter term Employment Insurance benefits, and so end up on the precarious work treadmill, going from one temporary or contract job to another. That is when many people become conscious of which side of the fence they are on and begin to understand who else is there with them.

When I lived with a close friend in the early 1990s, she—while being the single parent of two young children, living on social assistance and being forced to fight for the odd child support payment from the father—still identified herself as a white, middle-class woman. It sounds ludicrous now, but our brand of feminism at the time led us to a limited understanding of our social location. It's useful to look at this example using the analytical framework outlined earlier. In terms of understanding the everyday and structural racism and privilege, it is fair to say that we had a remorse-driven form of anti-racism. For example, our analysis of the dispossession of Aboriginal people just made us mostly feel really white and really bad; remorse-based anti-racism did not lead us to an analysis that would have integrated class and gender, not just in terms of the Aboriginal people we felt so bad about, but also for understanding our own location as working-class women. It would have been helpful to have been able to see that she enjoyed a freedom *from* rather than a freedom *to* kind of privilege that white working-class people often experience. For example, as a landed immigrant from western Europe, even with an accent, my friend did not have her documents requested when she applied for welfare. A one-pronged race analysis of this situation led her to feeling "lucky" and diminished her self-understanding that she was marginalized by poverty and by the oppressive state systems that pass for a social safety net. As well, a thorough analysis of how gender and class come together to sentence most single mothers to poverty would have led to different conclusions about her social location. Further, we were living in a period of intense neo-liberal restructuring, when the material and ideological assaults of today were just getting into high gear. Increased deregulation and corporate tax cuts were happening while the social assistance program was becoming more persecutory. The "Parental Support Unit" came into being at that time, the department that requires women on assistance to go after the fathers of their children for child support, or face losing the money from their monthly benefits cheque. This "mother persecution unit," as we called it, is but one example of how the evolution of capitalism to that point in history had a direct impact on our daily lives.

Given that ideological onslaught, who would want to proudly proclaim membership on the lower rungs of a highly fragmented working class, one in which those above you often hold you in disdain or see you as charity work? Combined with the social stigma created and maintained by elites, the lack of solidarity within the working class itself makes self-identification as a poor working-class woman a psychological condemnation to a lifetime of poverty. Saying we are middle class makes it temporary; it gives us hope.

White Privilege

Whiteness protected me from many kinds of hostility, distress, and violence, which I was being subtly trained to visit, in turn, upon people of colour.[15]

The fact that privilege is on the other side of the coin from oppression is difficult for some people on the left to accept. "White people who are aware of racial oppression seem to be less aware of race privilege. Whites tend to conceptualize race, racism and racist social structures as external to them, not as elements that shape them and their reality."[16] While we will accept the existence of white supremacy, seeing and personalizing how white privilege is a core part of that often doesn't come easily for us. Part of our privilege is not to even think of our whiteness, because we are not taught to recognize white privilege.

Part of the problem too is that this word "privilege" has become so morally loaded on the left. It can be used in such a limited way, causing us to silence ourselves and others in unhelpful ways. If we cannot get beyond "you/we need to deal with your/our privilege," then all we do is get stuck in guilt, either further avoiding dealing with racism at all or passively waiting to be told what to do. So we need to actively grapple in a much broader way with the reality of privilege as a set of social benefits.

Another aspect of that privilege is not having to experience the intense presence of the state in our lives as non-white people do.[17] For the most recent example, we have just to look at the terrorization of many people in Canada of Middle Eastern and South and West Asian descent over the last year. Sudden requests from immigration to review years'-old landing documents, refusals to allow boarding of airlines and arbitrary detentions without charge are some but not all of what is happening. As white leftists, we do despise the imperialist expansion of which these domestic racist attacks are an integral part but we are most unlikely to be targets. Even if somewhat perversely, even if it is, as mentioned above, in the form of that freedom *from* something, not a freedom *to do* something, this is a privilege.

A great deal of the white working-class's white supremacy is developed through ideological identification with the white ruling and middle classes. The privilege received as part of this relationship is in the form of tangible, material benefits such as better access to skilled, higher paying jobs, social freedom and economic means to have better housing than the rest of the working class.

The poorest of the white working class who have never been able to own a home, can barely pay the rent or can never go to university also share that ideological connection. Because of their class position, though, the material benefits are often quite limited. The benefit can be being less likely to get the worst jobs and housing or the privilege of simply not being a target of debilitating, everyday racism.

White supremacy has been so successful at establishing and maintaining white as "normal," in making this ideological connection that it is invisible to us in a most powerful way. We have become de-ethnicized and we either think we have no culture or that "Canadian culture" is "ours." The "invisible knapsack" metaphor for this phenomenon is appropriate.[18] Not all white privileges are inherently bad: it is just that they become privileges because non-white people are denied access to them. Here is a list of a few more examples, from both Peggy McIntosh and me:

- I can count on the neutrality of my neighbours in most places I live.

- I can open the paper or turn on the TV and see people who look like me, especially in positions of influence and power.

- I can do well in a difficult situation without being a credit to my "race."

- I can do poorly in a difficult situation without being a discredit to my "race."

- I am never asked to speak for and explain the experience of all whites.

- If a cop pulls me over or stops me on the street, it is not because of my "race."

- I will not get beaten, driven out of town, or murdered by the police because of the colour of my skin.

- When I drop off a job application and someone tells me the position is filled, I can be pretty sure it is true and not because of the colour of my skin.

- I can be silent about racism and I can avoid dealing with the unpleasantness of challenging racist incidents, ideas or legislation.

- As a white worker born in Canada, it is safe to assume that I permanently have a passport and other citizenship rights. In fact, I never have to think about it.

White privilege is often about making the choice of when or if to engage in struggle, as we higher waged white workers have with racism in the working class and in society in general. We can decide when or if to take on those "subtle Canadian" racist remarks of a coworker or another activist, or when or if to see the fight against racist policing as a single issue, not a campaign for global justice. We can slip in and out of the "mainstream" invisibly if we choose. And that is a powerful benefit to have, whether actively sought or passively received. For example, three years ago, I became a unionized worker for the first time in my life, in a rather conservative union. Because I engaged in the union, both with white and non-white unionists, I saw a kind of racism that made me say to fellow unionists and activists, "This is incredible; it's like the 1950s!" What I have been realizing though, is that, while the racism in that union was particularly overt and public at times, it was not a throwback to the 1950s. Women of colour I know and work with have been dealing every day for many years with the racist, sexist, heterosexist kind of crap I started seeing and hearing more recently. I was simply unfamiliar with being around it in such high dosages because as a higher waged, post-secondary-educated white worker and leftist, I had been able to structure into my life the choice not to engage with deeply, overtly racist white people. Enjoying this kind of privilege can make for poor white anti-racism.

While enjoying privilege is not inevitable or natural, we live like this in a mutually reinforcing agreement among white people in the ruling, middle and working classes. Historically, this cross-class collusion can be seen, for example, in the fact that non-white women's hard labour has allowed middle-class women to be home with their children when they choose to and supported them (e.g. through migrant nannies) when they go out to professional jobs. The privileged access that working-class white women have to the higher waged work often means a climb right out of the working class.

Even at the best of times, when white leftists can see our privilege, we often see it as some sort of monolithic, one-dimensional power base from which to bring people together and to then transmit skills, abilities and ideas. This is when taking responsibility can become taking over.

The State

We think of those with political power in Canada as the government, made up of representatives of parties that we vote for every few years. The institutions that these politicians take their seats in and make their living from are seen as neutral bodies, as elected overseers of ministries or departments that deliver social programs. So, it then becomes everyone's responsibility (those with the right to vote, that is) to participate in "our democracy" and vote ourselves in a "good government" from a supposed wide array of choices.

However, this set of institutions is not neutral and not just about health care and education. Collectively it is part of the state, which has a very specific role in propelling ruling class interests. It has been historically essential for the development of capitalism in Canada. That is, the "political formation of the nation-state," plus the "capitalist relations of production," historically come together to build and reproduce the "imagined community"[19] — that basic, mythical notion of who "we" are together as "a people" — in the face of ongoing resistance, contradictions and economic crises.

The state's specific functions include guaranteeing private property, making sure business has access to ever-cheaper and "flexible" labour supplies, creating the social climate within which all this happens and keeping the social order. As mentioned above, non-white people are subjected to the "pervasive presence of the state"[20] in their lives, ranging from immigration and citizenship rights control, to access to work, to targeted policing. The brutal racist harassment and murders of Aboriginal people and people of colour by police is an enduring reality.[21] As such, systemic racism is part of the nation-state political process, not just something running through institutions or organizations that is separate from that process.

Since a key foundation for Canadian state development was and is white supremacy, and since it has not been politically helpful for the ruling class for some years to continue with its overt "white man's country" policy of ruling and settlement, the state has evolved its mode of racist organization to suit the new political times. As we'll see later, multiculturalism policy and practice has been indispensable recently in creating and maintaining a liberal mask for white supremacy.

Social Relations
Most basically, "social relations" are patterned interactions between groups of people. Looking at social relations shows us how various forms of power are formed, become systemic, are carried out over time, and how they overlap and interconnect. Racism, sexism and class exploitation are relations that, over time, come from processes of domination and struggles over which groups get to control the means of production (machinery, factories and banks) and how this control is set up and

continued in our society. Racism as a social relation evolved not just by the action of the state but of the working class as well, and not just by white workers' embracing and implementing racism but also by non-white peoples' resistance to it. The variation of the forms of systemic racism and other social relations affects our agency, our ability to fight back collectively in different ways at different times.

Non-White People and People of Colour

As Enakshi Dua spells out, "In Canada there is little consensus among anti-racist feminist writers on how to name those groups that have been marginalized by racialization."[22] There are two terms that seem to be most common, though: "non-white women/people" and "women/people of colour." I know and know of women of colour who object to one or the other term, and some who reject or can generally live with both. People I know who reject "non-white" have said they don't want to be defined by what they are not, whereas those who embrace the term do so because it puts whiteness front and centre. The former folks will often say that "of colour" is preferred because it came from people of colour as a progressive alternative to the racist "coloured people." Those who are uncomfortable with the term often see little difference between the new version and the racist old one. Since there is no easy answer, I will use both terms.

Capitalization also varies. I capitalize when using specific cultural or national designations. Since First Nations or Aboriginal people occupy a specific location in racist Canadian society, the term "people of colour" is not generally used as inclusive of them. However, unless I make a specific point about Aboriginal people, the terms "non-white" and "of colour" will be inclusive.

Far Left and Left

When we say someone is on "the left," this can mean many things. It can range from someone for whom getting the Kyoto Accord signed represents a major step towards social change, to those who see revolution as the only way to end capitalist exploitation and oppression. For my purposes here, when I say the "left," I will be referring generally to both a person or group who seeks any kind of social change to improve conditions of life, and those who want complete social transformation. If I am only referring to those who want to fundamentally transform society, be it by revolution or some other program they have in mind, I will use the term "far left." This is necessary to be specific yet avoid getting lost in political differences among those who are anarchists, anti-oppression feminists, various kinds of socialists, Marxists, communists and/or anti-capitalists. Those political distinctions are important, yet spelling them all out in detail is not needed here.

3

An Anti-Racist Feminist Look At Canadian Racism's History

Introduction

In 1990, the Oka, Quebec, City Council hired a developer to construct another nine-hole golf course and some condos. The site chosen for this development was Mohawk land, building on which would destroy a burial ground and many old pine trees. The federal government refused to meet and negotiate with the Mohawks as equals, as even Canadian law would seem to require. Instead the Quebec provincial police — Sureté du Quebec — and the Canadian military were sent in, armed to the teeth. With many women in the lead, the resistance of the people of Kanehsatake and other supporting Mohawk communities that ensued became known across Canada and internationally as a battle for basic recognition of Aboriginal land and self-determination rights. Even with Quebec's ongoing subordination to English Canada, the state response at

Oka showed how "Europeans continue the same solidarity of ruling and repression, blended with competitive manipulations, that they practised from the dawn of their conquests and state formation."[1] At the same time, for many white activists such as myself, this was an inspiring struggle to behold and get behind.

Looking at the deep roots of the history of white racism in the development of the Canadian state and, by association, Canadian capitalism, seems like an important next step in our journey to understanding how to better get behind and/or get into anti-racist organizing. But, is it always the key to better anti-racism, given that some people know a lot about history yet do little to use that knowledge in the present?

Just knowing a history is not enough to make us do anything different in the present, but it can lay a foundation for change. An anti-racist feminist point of view is critical to making women and men of colour visible to whites, to make us really see non-white people around us as they are instead of through our various stereotypes and assumptions. Our mainstream present and history have taught us the opposite. Note how the Canadian state's strange term "visible minority" — created in the mid-1980s as part of its response to the organizing of women of colour — can still be employed in Toronto today when non-white people are the majority! Seeing the long and complex history of Aboriginal people and people of colour here in Canada starts to shake loose all those other images of brave white pioneers battling the elements and savages, to challenge the ideas and stories that continue to support the false, yet all too firm, foundation for whites' sense of place and entitlement.

In addition, an anti-racist feminist perspective on the past that is also socialist puts Aboriginal women and women of colour's lives, both their oppression and resistance, in the forefront of the analysis of racist capitalist development in Canada. With such a perspective, we can start to see history as a complex process that involves actions of various peoples within different kinds of systems, not just a linear chain of events with dates attached. We can then start to see the labour of working-class women of colour as the backbone of the international economy, their disproportionately low wages and poor working conditions as a major source of the runaway profits of corporations, banks and a relative few individuals. Gaining this perspective allows us to see non-white women as actively involved in life, as subjects, rather than seeing them as being on the bottom rung of some inevitable economic ladder from which, by our good will and intentions, we can only hope to pull them up a few steps.

But why an anti-racist feminist *socialist* perspective? Socialism in our day and age has been widely discredited due to many factors. For one thing, it is the failure of self-described socialist revolutions or reformations around the world to create truly democratic and egalitarian societies. In the wake of those disappointments, socialism, for many, has become synonymous with Stalin's brutal Soviet regime of the twentieth century, North Korea's and China's ongoing fierce authoritarian governing, as well as Cuba's own brand of communism. While the left bears a great weight of historical responsibility for the state we are in, the right has played no small part. When the Berlin Wall came down in 1989, British Prime Minister Margaret Thatcher gleefully proclaimed the world's entry into the era of "there is no alternative" (TINA) to capitalism.[2] Socialism had apparently failed and "democracy" (used interchangeably by elites for "capitalism" and/or "imperialism") was free to rule. However, as some socialists had long argued, these were not, in fact, socialist societies. They were bureaucractic dictatorships in which a ruling class made up of the top state and party officials exploited the labour of working people while twisting the words of Marx to justify a social order that suited them.

Even though unpopular and often mocked, socialist analyses and aspirations do still live on and have an important place in anti-racist work. My socialism is about materially valuing human lives and potential above the value of profits and products. It's about building a society on the basis of justice, dignity and respect, not on the basis of class-, race- and gender-based hierarchies that allow a few in power to dictate the terms of existence for the many. Even if it's a challenging time to do so, if we look seriously at the historical complexity of social relations and, therefore, at the multiple levels at which we must integrate our analysis and action, then we can see that grassroots socialist ideas and practice are as important today as they were in the last century.

Following is a look at the process of white nation-building in the context of colonization and the development of imperialism and capitalism. Many sources give a fuller review of this legacy of destruction and death. This effort is not meant to repeat in detail those historical accounts; rather, it is to focus specifically on how racism has developed in Canada, how different non-white groups were affected by it, all intertwined with the complex evolution of other social relations. Maintaining our focus on people's agency as well as on the structures within which we are struggling is key to a good integrated analysis that will help point the way to better organizing. A key part of that agency is the historical resistance of people of colour to racism, because that history is as long as the oppression itself.

Othering and Christianity, Race and Racism: The Chickens and the Eggs

> Canadians did not invent "race": it was the product of a global paradigm emerging from European expansion and conquest.[3]

When looking at the historical roots of racism, we often get stuck in making a case for what the actual starting point was. For example, the argument is often made that racism did not start until coherent ideas of race existed. Given that the word "race" was used in Ireland in a 1317 manifesto to describe how England's laws were designed and practised to exterminate the Irish,[4] could that be the starting point? Or is it not until the development of scientific theories in the eighteenth century that helped justify the earlier enslavement of Africans in this hemisphere?

I don't want to suggest an original or specific starting point for racism. Instead, I want to show that there was a logic to the process of white supremacy and racism development that pre-dated capital's specific need for labour, and that there is historical continuity between the centuries of "othering" before the racism that developed as part of the European colonial expansion that led to capitalist development. This does not mean that the xenophobia of 1000 years ago is the same as the racism of today; it does mean, though, that there is a significant historical connection between the everyday and structural forms of previous time periods and today.

Over thousands of years, migration has brought people of different physical appearances, cultural norms and behaviour into contact with one another. In the process of trying to explain such differences, human beings would create "'representations' of the Other, images and beliefs which categorise people in terms of real or attributed differences when compared with Self."[5] In the context of colonization, this process of "othering" became infused with power, changing the significance of such differences and how these differences were used to oppress and exploit.

Europe only became known as such in the eighth century and much of it was under Arab political, economic and military domination until at least the 1300s. The fifteenth century Greco-Roman cultural influence on laying down whiteness as positive and blackness as negative is an important historical forerunner of racism today. Christianity then deepened and refined this with the literal use of the bible to explain the world, such that certain physical features and colour symbolism were reinforced and extended to code non-white people as monstrous, sinful and sexually aggressive, people who could threaten social control within ideal Christian life, especially those "wild savages" outside their borders.[6]

Nation-state development in northwestern Europe started in the fifteenth century. By the time the upper-class European explorers of the sixteenth and seventeenth centuries were to set out on their missions of travel, trade and takeover, they were so steeped in the othering tradition — and its use for gaining class domination — that the colonization project was well primed for racism and for white supremacy. That is, in the process of setting up Aboriginal people and Africans as "savages," the Europeans' economic and intellectual elites were constructing themselves as "civilized," part of what later became known as the supposed Manifest Destiny of whites.[7]

A significant part of the brutality of colonization and domination involved using various methods of forcing Christianity on Aboriginal and other non-white people for social control. The continuity of connection between religion and both ethnic discrimination and racism has a long and complex history. Even within Christianity, conversion to escape oppression had often been only selectively promoted to the propertied or professional Irish Catholics by the Irish Protestant ruling class (the Protestant Ascendancy) in seventeenth-century Ireland.[8] English ruling-class use of religion for repressive treatment of the Irish also "laid crucial building blocks for racism as a belief system."[9] This belief system was well applied to justify the nineteenth-century shift into the high gears of empire building, as the world's main capitalist powers violently competed for new and existing colonized territories. Yet, it was laid down even before the institutionalization of slavery in the US, so religious conversion was not an automatic road to freedom from oppression and it was already integrated with class. And the less you were associated with both the "goodness" of whiteness and the more you resisted colonizers' attempts to subjugate you for their purposes, the less likely conversion would improve your circumstances, as the many Aboriginal Christians living on impoverished reserves today can report. Their ancestors' forced or coerced conversion did not free them from oppression; it deepened it. Since conversion was for control, a similar thing happened with Africans.[10]

One example of the complex role of Christianity in Canadian colonialism is that of early nineteenth-century Protestant missionary work in Upper Canada.[11] As in other parts of what was to become Canada, missionary goals were intertwined with those of imperial expansion. Missionaries believed that moving from a hunting and gathering way of life to an agriculturally based settled life was key to redemption. Of course, this shift was also a key requirement of capitalist development in the colony. The persistent colonial imagery and discourse of Aboriginals as barbarians was an important tool to this end, used in conjunction with such things as Aboriginal-targeted calls for temperance and a push to force Native women into the more pious, less "wild" role of homemaker. These tools were applied to change over time how people thought and felt about themselves, for themselves and in relation to each other. Power, then, is clearly not just about the ability to forceably take land; it's also more insidiously about forceably transforming people's subjectivity.

During the "course of colonization," a tighter and tighter link was drawn between wildness and dark skin, and "these representations increasingly refracted a new purpose as discovery was followed by settlement, and settlement by the introduction of systems of unfree labour."[12] The representations had become more complex in the seventeenth and eighteenth centuries — when most Europeans knew Africans as slaves — as wildness became bestiality and the myth of the potent sexuality of both non-white women and men was played up.

As culture was secularized and science gained a foothold as a way of rationally understanding and organizing the world, Europeans started to use scientific criteria in the late eighteenth century to transform othering into a supposedly objective separation of humanity into various "races" with apparently ever-essentialized biological characteristics (ranging from head size and shape to skin colour) that further justified ranking humanity in a hierarchy of importance and therefore of powerless and powerful. In Europe, this justification helped explain the contradiction of deepening social inequality in the face of Enlightenment values: natural equality was replaced with natural differences.[13] In colonized territories like the US and Canada, it was used to justify the enslavement, the sub-human treatment, of thousands of Africans.

While ideas that underpin this scientific racism have largely been discredited in our time and place, they still structure everyday understandings about the Other, as "it is still widely assumed that 'races' exist as distinct, biologically defined collectivities."[14] We now have a mix of implicit biological and explicit cultural bases for racism that use the notions of natural "cultural difference" to slot people into racial and ethnic groups[15] and to mask racism. We now must deal with an overlap of scientific and cultural explanations.[16] Given this, we can see how the idea of race developed for social reasons, socially constructing the Other on the basis of white supremacy.[17] While we continue to challenge the validity of the idea of dividing humanity on the basis of this idea, it is equally important to emphasize the very real material base that the concept of race has in the lives of many people as the foundation of multiple forms of racism: race has become a social reality.

This analysis takes a starting point for the development of racism that is different from several of the sources looked at in the coming chapter, as well as others. That is, many arguments on racism's development by the far left tend to be functionalist: rather than an analysis that shows how racism's development is indeed relevant to capitalism's development and also became integrated with it, a functionalist explanation says that racism was invented by capitalists because they needed the inferiority of people of colour for the needs of capitalism.

It is often said that racism came out of slavery, because of the unfree labour needed for cash cropping and other large-scale resource rip-offs, and it was Africans who were enslaved because they were "cheap labour," not because they were Black. But how is it that they became cheaper than the Irish, if that is the case?[18] If racism came from using white servitude as the model for Black enslavement, if it was such a good model, why stop enslaving the Irish and move entirely to large-scale Black slavery in a worse form than the white one, and make such an allowance for improved white working-class Irish conditions? If the practice was only to create a "buffer group,"[19] why is it that, in historical circumstances of the period and place looked at here, non-white people never had access to the privileged position of the Irish?

A thing's function does not necessarily explain its origins.[20] Saying that the origins of racism pre-date slavery does not deny that racism's roots and ongoing maintenance have had real economic, political and social benefits for the rulers and detriments for the targets. Whereas, to say that racism started with race "detaches history from its roots."[21] That is, racial oppression pre-dates the eighteenth century ideology of race. How we understand that history becomes important when we see some of the consequences for white leftists' relationship to racism today. Functionalist ways of looking at racism can lead us to understand social structures as the entire roots and branches of racism, leaving out white people's involvement in benefiting from and maintaining all the aspects of systemic racism. This then deeply affects how we go about our organizing.

White Nation-Building as People Live, Migrate and Settle

The people of Canada want to have a white country.[22]

So said Prime Minister Wilfrid Laurier in 1914. With the infamous exception of former Toronto Mayor Mel Lastman, such overt expressions of white supremacy by state leaders are almost unheard-of today because of how the implementation of white racism has had to change in response to non-white peoples' resistance and capital's needs. But 100 years ago, Laurier and his fellow travellers had every confidence in uttering such statements to promote their white nation-building agenda because it was not just a few ruling-class members' ideas that were being promoted: it was, by then, the law of the land. The White Canada Policy officially implemented through the 1910 Immigration Act was put in place to ideologically and materially expand the ruling class idea of the "imagined community." It contained explicit definitions of who was "desirable" and who was not, the latter including nationalities with "peculiar customs" and "methods of holding property" that made them unassimilable.[23] All this was continuous with pre-twentieth-century racist colonial roots.

Imperialism, Capitalism and Aboriginal-European Relations

There is a wide range of views on the nature of the early relationships between Europeans and Aboriginal people, what Sarah Carter usefully terms a debate between the romantics and the rationalists.[24] The romantics tend towards an overly generous view of Aboriginal peoples' autonomy and self-determination in the course of European contact and colonial expansion. Their focus on Aboriginal agency often appears to be at the cost of denying the way the developing interracial social relations meant there were complex and contradictory impacts of contact with and colonization by Europeans. The rationalists, on the other hand, err in the other direction, objectifying Aboriginal people, denying them agency in that new and developing social reality, as those historians overemphasize the destructive imposition of European beliefs and technologies.

To honour Aboriginal people's activity, roles and the positive benefits they received from the relationship with Europeans in the early days of the creation of today's society does not mean we deny the exploitation and oppression created by the colonial and imperialist activity of Britain and France. As colonization started globally, the often brutal contact with indigenous populations was ultimately about competing for land, establishing private property rights, getting a labour force under control and foisting Christianity on people in the process. In Canada, there was an initial strategy of working out trade and other agreements with Aboriginal peoples because such "relations of interdependence" were easier as long as control was asserted and the goal of extracting profit was met;[25] it was easier largely due to the often sophisticated resistance of Aboriginal people. An example of such an agreement is the 1664 Two-Row Wampum Treaty between the Iroquois Nation and the British. But there were differences between the gradual assimilation strategy of the French versus the more coercive methods of the British that were a result of their different domestic histories of imperialist and capitalist development, which led to their initial differing goals and needs for colonization.[26]

More so than any other Western nation, "the development of capitalism at home in Britain determined the shape of British imperialism."[27] The roots of this are found in Britain's particular history of agrarian capitalist development, through which the ideology of valuing land based on the economic value that could be extracted from it was put into place through the large-scale dispossession of rural peasants so that the land could be "improved." As the ideology and need for land developed hand in hand, any land not being actively developed for the purpose of profit extraction was deemed to be in a state of "waste." As landlords acquired land to start focussing on the generation of commercial profits, the massive population displaced in this process had to go somewhere. And colonial expansion was ultimately just the place to put them.

France, on the other hand, had a less specifically capitalist approach to its imperial development in terms of the orientation towards property and how to expand control and wealth. As a result, it maintained a majority peasant population and so had no "surplus population" to turn to as the English did. Further, it was less ideologically extreme in taking over "unused land." The French seemed to believe that Aboriginal people did legitimately inhabit some land, while they merely "roamed" over other areas. As such, it was enough that they were *using* the land; they didn't have to be *improving* it, as the British ideology held.

Given these differences, we can see why the French might have been more interested in taking hold of the fur trade in British North America while the English, although involved in the fur trade, might have been more intent on taking over as much "unoccupied" land as possible. In fact, the latter unabashedly used the 1670 establishment of the Hudson's Bay Company as a vehicle for territorial claim.[28] Further, we can also see how their imperialist pursuits were connected with the different forms and intensity of racist treatment of Aboriginal people. The initially less brutal, relationship-building methods of the French could have had more to do with the initially less capitalist character of France's imperialism than a better approach to human relations.

Especially with the French, then, the fur trade was critical to the nature of early Aboriginal and European relations. From 1670 to 1870, this was a form of "commodity exchange between Europeans and Native peoples, and it required much more extensive and sustained contact between" them.[29] Europeans came to rely on Aboriginal people for their multiple roles in facilitating European involvement in the pre-existing, extensive Aboriginal trade networks. At the same time, Aboriginal people gained access to European technologies. As Carter states in reference to the success of the 200-year fur trade enterprise, during which time the Europeans were integrated, "The success of this industry required the cooperation of both parties ... (a)lthough it was not an equal partnership ... (but) a mutual dependence that was qualitatively different for each side. Europeans were dependent ultimately only for profits and always had the option of quitting the business altogether."[30]

While Aboriginal women often did unpaid labour in dressing furs and making food or canoes, they also worked as guides and interpreters on trips. Many of these activities were not new to the Aboriginal trade relationship with the colonizers and the act of performing them did not make the women (or men) subordinate. Rather, it was the change in the production process as well as the sale for profit that was significant in the relationships with colonial powers. For example, beaver pelts had always been valuable to Aboriginal people, but once they became a commodity for sale, "an impulse to harvest beyond the limits established in traditional conservationist practice" was introduced, leading to what "may have been the first time ... scarcity ... was created by overharvesting."[31] Scarcity then generated further competition and supported the existing environment of conflict created by the colonizers. But scarcity and competition did not necessarily bring with them a drive for profit by Aboriginal people. The Aboriginal concept of making a gain from the fur trade pre-dated colonial contact, but their motive for making a surplus was opposite to that of the colonizers: Aboriginal people did not try to get more money for furs so they could buy more goods; they did it to meet their needs with less effort.

Despite the historical differences in the origins of imperialism, as time went on, the dominant practice for both powers became one of methodical "racist and genocidal policies and practices (designed) to obliterate whole Indigenous societies and cultures."[32] Initially this was through "military action and disease, the latter of which saw 90% of the Americas' Aboriginal population decimated after 20 waves of pestilence."[33] Smallpox was catastrophic for Aboriginal people. Later attacks were by legislation, but the devastation brought by disease and Christianity became intertwined with that brought by trade.[34] As the two invading nations fought out the terms of their co-existence, which ended up in "a relationship of conquest and domination with each other,"[35] all other inhabitants became excluded, in often contradictory ways, from having any self-determining, powerful role in the development of the colonies that would later become the Canadian state.[36]

Interracial Relationships

The varying attitudes towards interracial relationships between white settler men and Aboriginal women are an example of contradictions in ruling-class domination. Sometimes, such relationships were encouraged and, at others, discouraged, often by the same colonial representatives.

For example, encouraging marriage of Aboriginal women to working-class French settlers assisted in the process of "securing female submission,"[37] to populate the colonies and to provide "knowledge, skills and familial comforts"[38] to men in fur production. But it also had benefits to Aboriginal women, bringing potentially greater economic security as a result of the many benefits Europeans in turn received from these relationships. Yet, the more competitive and the more profitable the fur trade became, the more Aboriginal women became exploited and abused, and the more likely it was for men to marry mixed or white women.

In what is now northern Ontario, interracial common-law relationships, or "marriage à la façon du pays," were a social reality of the era. Initially most acceptable and desirable to the French, these relationships and the broad familial connections coming out of them, uncommon in North America as a whole, became an integral part of all of western Canada's fur trade society, and were often vigorously challenged by Christian missionaries.[39]

Not all missionaries, however. While Catholic and Protestant missionaries in northern Ontario and Manitoba contributed to Aboriginal women's social dislocation as legitimate wives of white men,[40] BC missionaries saw Christian inter-marriage in the late nineteenth century as a way to try to control the cohabitation of white men and Aboriginal women, a widespread social phenomenon that caused them and the rest of the colonizing class great concern.[41] The missionaries did not see the interracial relationships as desirable, particularly because Aboriginal women were not Christian, but great pains were taken to try to clamp down on the more socially relaxed and free-flowing interracial, working-class relationships, which ultimately could not be controlled. The "civilizing" function of marriage was one tactic to achieve this. An additional benefit of inter-marriage was that white men could act as colonizers in their own homes. Interestingly, further east, inter-marriage had an unexpected repercussion for resistance, as the resulting Métis descendants thought of themselves as a new nation with legitimate claims to land.[42]

At the same time as the church in BC was trying to use marriage as a last resort, BC employers also acted to discourage such interracial marriages because of their fear of the loss, through racial mixing, of the superiority they believed whiteness had. To this end, Aboriginal women were demonized ideologically as drunks and prostitutes, the "dark, mirror image to the idealized nineteenth-century visions of white women,"[43] and excluded legally and physically through health campaigns and legislative efforts at urban racial segregation.

Getting Control of Land and Resources:
Continued Attacks on People and the Environment

Across what is now Canada, the colonizers' central purpose in applying such contradictory forms of domination was to develop the means of production. Even as far back as 1627 to 1643, more French-Catholic men were sought to shift the economy from the emphasis on the fur trade to one that required settlers, "based on lumbering, mining, fishing, manufacturing, and trade with the West Indies, all of which required the importation of capital, managerial talent and skilled labour,"[44] as the French ruling class took on more of the British form in colonial domination. Ongoing settlement — particularly by importing white working-class Europeans and attempting to force settlement of Aboriginal people for subjugation and assimilation — and the control of Aboriginal land were key to the needs of agriculturally based capitalist development: land and a labour force.[45]

From the early days of Confederation, when the newly official Canadian ruling class began stepping up its capitalist expansion, the Grassy Narrows First Nation located in northwestern Ontario has been trying to hold on to their territory and way of life. There is a trail of dishonour, and both human and environmental degradation, that leads from the signing of Treaty 3 in 1873 to the early 1990s installation of Abitibi-

Consolidated in the Whiskey Jack forest, on Grassy territory, in order to massively clear-cut and continue to expand the forest industry owners' profits. On that 100-year path is the early destruction of the sturgeon fishery by white commercial fishers; an 1881 Indian Act amendment prohibiting "western Indians" (Treaty 3 people included) from selling agricultural produce, so their wild rice, potatoes and corn wouldn't compete with white capitalist agricultural expansion; the early and mid-twentieth-century rapid expansion of logging, mining, hydro-electric projects, and later, the development of tourist lodges and the cottage industry, in which Aboriginal people were largely excluded from waged work; and the 1970s extensive mercury poisoning of water by Dryden Pulp and Paper Company's mill, with the resulting major health problems and high unemployment for Grassy Narrows and Whitedog First Nations, as the major source of employment for Aboriginal people was the commercial fishery. As a result of historical and ongoing attacks on their lives, the local people started a blockade of the logging road at Grassy Narrows in December 2002, after a decade of official government protest that fell on deaf ears at both federal and provincial levels.[46]

The history of land expropriation and attacks on the self-governance of the Kahienkehaka (Mohawk) Nation is also a long one. "Since Haudenosaunee (Iroquois) women owned the land, to dispossess and expropriate Haudenosaunee lands, the colonizers had to eradicate the political power of women"[47] as well as deal with the military strength of the Iroquois people as a whole. This was generally the case in other Aboriginal societies as well, where "women were considerably freer in matters of work, sexuality and political influence than their counterparts in seventeenth-century Europe."[48] Aboriginal women were often the backbone of their communities.[49] This status of women made it very difficult to use religious conversion, inter-marriage or forced wage labour to divide and colonize Aboriginal people. During early days of colonization, Aboriginal women often refused to give up rights they had had long before the colonizers came, such as those of divorce and agricultural control. They held out against religious conversion, they resisted the Christian marriage the missionaries tried to force on them and some refused to let their daughters go to mission schools. And so goes the Cheyenne proverb: "A nation is not conquered until the hearts of its women are on the ground."[50]

Everything visited upon Aboriginal women by the forces of colonization was designed to "reduce (them) to powerless and depersonalized objects of scorn."[51] One result of this was the legal, social and economic exclusion of most women and an associated impoverishment. (It also made a lie of the lives of the majority of non-white and white women who were working class and did hard work on farms, in family businesses or in households, including that of having and caring for children.) The combination of racist laws and other means of control and displacement that were carried out from the end of the nineteenth century into the twentieth left many Aboriginal women and men in poverty. To add to the cruelty, the state used this fact as an excuse for further brutal paternalism and state intervention.

Slavery and Migration:
Another Chapter in White Nation Building

Given the difficulty of Aboriginal enslavement[52] and the legality of that of Africans, Black slavery was alive and well in Canada in the 1600 and 1700s.[53] Then, in the late 1700s, an ethnic mix of United Empire Loyalists came to Canada. Among them were 3000 Blacks who were freed on the condition they fight with the British. Many went to Nova Scotia where they found "what was to become a pervasive pattern of anti-black racism and segregation,"[54] without access to the land and liberty of white loyalists. At the same time, many Black women found their freedom to be elusive, still being treated as property after slavery officially ended.[55]

In fact, historian Sylvia Hamilton says the first Canadian race riot was in 1784 in Shelburne, NS, when white soldiers tried to drive free

Blacks out by burning down their homes. This response to "cheap" Black labour would continue even after 1880 when many Maroons (descendants of runaway Jamaican slaves) and other Black settlers would sail for Sierra Leone. As well, "40–60,000 fugitive slaves and free Blacks fled to what is now Ontario between 1815–1860."[56]

African-Canadian resistance to racism has been strong since as early as the 1600s and 1700s. A few examples are Marie-Joseph Angelique who burned down forty-six buildings in Montréal when she found out she was going to be sold,[57] Lydia Jackson's resistance in Nova Scotia to a "depraved indifference to (her) humanity," and the more well-known heroine of the underground railroad, Harriet Tubman. It was the determined action of slaves themselves that led to anti-slavery court challenges and so the official, legal end of slavery in Upper Canada in 1833. It was Black voters who protested when a Toronto city councillor insisted in 1864 on referring to them as n—ers.

By 1867, two-thirds of the population of British North America was of western European origin.[58] Between 1846 and 1854, 400,000 Irish came, due to starvation and because the British wanted to get rid of this domestic imperial problem. Most men worked mainly in canal construction and the shipping industry, but a large number of these migrants were single women who came because the lack of industrial development in Ireland made the chances for waged work slim, and the lack of access to land (due to British imperialism) made marriage opportunities few and far between.[59]

Working as domestic servants for the colonial ruling class, these women experienced ethnic discrimination based on stereotypes of Irish women as being "good-hearted but dim." However, their treatment because of attitudes towards their working class location was even worse: their very public life as single women going out drinking clashed head on with the Victorian ideology of femininity, the "cult of womanhood," that was actively introduced in the early nineteenth century in all colonized territories, which promoted racial purity through an ideal (white) femininity as "fragile, virtuous and subservient."[60] Harsh punishment was meted out to domestic workers caught drunk in public: there were more women incarcerated than men between 1856 and 1865, specifically on charges of public drunkenness, and "increasing incarcerations coincided with the particularly zealous efforts of Toronto officials to define and regulate behaviour on the streets and other public places within this prosperous, industrializing provincial capital."[61]

As we see from the treatment of both those present and migrating, the task of nation-building for capitalist development also then became about building and maintaining class structure, which is intertwined with sexism and racism. The history of the Canadian state shows the dynamic and often nasty nature of the evolution of these interconnected social relations. The phase of Canadian nation-building of from 1880 to 1920 required both development of the physical infrastructure for capitalism (for example, a manufacturing base and transportation system) and a focus on the human nation. Nation-state development tools include negotiation, force and the "active creation of myths about historical origin and tradition,"[62] and values to create the imagined community. Key to this was the mentioned Victorian ideology of womanhood.

The importation of white women in the nineteenth century helped to discourage white-Native marriage and encourage an environment of racist sexism in relation to an awareness of different class locations. And so the ruling class cultivated middle-class white women's cross-gender and class alliances with white men to assist in Aboriginal women's oppression. White British women and children were actively and aggressively sought to ensure the dominance of white Anglo-Saxons and, therefore, the ongoing implementation of these white supremacist, Victorian values. The racist attitudes developed in Britain by the ideology of British imperialism's "civilizing mission"[63] were carried over in the invisible knapsacks of British immigrants of various class backgrounds who actively participated in reproducing a hostile racist environment, not just for Aboriginal people but also for Blacks in early twentieth-century Canada from coast to coast. The importation of ruling and middle class British women aided in carrying out the multi-layered subordination of working-class white and non-white women. Such women were actively involved in immigration control in the nineteenth century. It was an effective contradiction, the pure, defenseless, white woman who nonetheless "aided in the defilement and exploitation of the colonized, in particular, of the colonized women."[64] This debasement has not been limited to Aboriginal women but has also been directed towards South Asian, African and Arab women, portraying them as originating from barbaric cultures, being highly "sexualized, cloistered, or both."[65] Part of white women's ongoing involvement in this contradictory representation and treatment was the threat they felt by the capability and relative self-sufficiency of Aboriginal women.

The non-gender-specific parts of the white nation rhetoric are found in the Canadian mask of white supremacy that persists today; that is, the white, Anglo-Saxon "claim to liberal values of 'individualism', 'truth', 'universalism', 'history', 'free speech', and 'freedom of expression,'"[66] values the "others" outside this discourse cannot share. By the early nineteenth century, this myth of the existence of an Anglo-Saxon race that could use these inherent qualities for the creation of democratic institutions worldwide was well established. As such, the imagination of white supremacy had been popularized for nation-state development. Today, the state-promoted Canadian nationalism that infuses the (white) population, regardless of class, with notions of being "civilized" and "modern," one that paints this country as a neutral, peace keeping, law-abiding state, also masks its global position as a small yet important imperialist power.[67]

To get to where we are today, the state also armed itself with legal powers that supported the ideology of white supremacy. The Royal Proclamation of 1763 started the "legal extortion of Aboriginal lands."[68] As part of the industrial capitalist project, British political institutions were cloned through the British North America Act of 1867, thereby legally and politically institutionalizing the nation-state's purpose as that of pursuing British Empire interests. The 1876 Indian Act refined Britain's rule of Aboriginal lands, and a litany of other repressive measures, and converted First Nations peoples into wards of the state. To appease the French elite, the British and French colonizers cut ongoing deals that led to an officially bicultural nation at Confederation, ignoring and excluding First Nations. "As a result, three categories of citizens were recognized: English Canadians, French Canadians and 'others.' Only the first two groups had constitutional rights"[69] and the French were subordinated to the English. And, similarly to how the Indian Act has excluded First Nations people internally, immigration law and policy have controlled migrants from entering and once they arrive.[70]

The 1911 exclusion of African-Americans' migration was attempted by an Order-in-Council that used the well-established racist representation of Black men as sexually violent towards white women in order for it to be passed.[71] While the Order was never implemented, the racist damage was done as the debate played out in western Canadian media. Many remarks, such as that of a Manitoba Tory who said "he wanted a 'white west' and urged the government to stop the flow of blacks,"[72] were published in the Alberta press. In contrast, we have seen how positive stereotyping of some white migrants opened doors for them.

Working-class Chinese migrants were also targeted by specific racist and sexist immigration policies as well as by employers' and unions' practices[73] in the late 1800s and early 1900s. The conditions in garment factories where many worked were and are often still horrible. Yet, "through their fight against anti-Chinese laws and practices, Chinese-Canadian women and men were successful in winning reunification of their families, enfranchisement for Chinese-Canadians, as well as improving working conditions."[74] Chinese workers were part of strikes dating from the 1860s, even before the overall increase in labour militancy after World War One. Because many Chinese were discriminated against in unemployment too, in the depression they became ineligible for relief available to other workers. As 135 Chinese-Vancouver men starved to death between 1932 and 1935, Chinese workers held demonstrations against this racist social program exclusion.

In the late nineteenth and early twentieth centuries, Ukrainians and Scandinavians were also recruited as free agricultural workers while the Chinese workers came "through an indentured labour system to build the railways for Canada's westward expansion."[75] Within this interaction of free and indentured working people — an unequally structured interaction created by the ruling class — the flames of white working-class supremacy and racism were fanned: they saw Chinese workers as "cheap and coerced" labour that could bring down better white conditions and wages.[76] In fact, the Chinese workers earned "½ to ¼ less than unskilled white men" in the same industries and were "denied the legal and political rights enjoyed by others in Canada."[77] It is estimated that Canada Pacific Railway saved $5,000,000 by exploiting Chinese labour.[78]

An exorbitant fifty dollar "head tax" (an immigration fee) was imposed on Chinese railway workers if they wanted to stay in Canada. Even if they could pay, they had no citizenship rights. From 1924–1947, there was a ban on Chinese immigration. All this made it almost impossible for Chinese women to migrate, other than the wives of the Chinese ruling class and clergy, or indentured servants or sex-trade workers. Women from all over Asia were so restricted in their ability to migrate that "by 1912 there were no more than 2,000 Asian women in Canada."[79] Dua relates the legal-political debate at the time about the so-called "Hindu Women's Question" that centred on whether migration of South Asian women — and then only as wives of South Asian men — was a threat to the moral and social order, a menace to the whiteness of the nation-building project. However, although representatives of the state held that position, middle- and ruling-class white women (such as members of the Imperial Order of the Daughters of the Empire) advocated for South Asian wives' migration due to their underlying fear that South Asian men's sexuality would be directed towards white women if South Asian wives were not present. While apparently opposite ends of a debate, both white arguments came from white supremacy's drive for racial purity.

Fleeing "viscious anti-Semitism and deepening poverty" in Tsarist Russia, Poland, Romania and the Austro-Hungarian Empire, almost 200,000 Jewish migrants came to Canada between 1891 and 1930, a third of whom found work in Toronto's needle trades.[80] Since they came with the intention to stay, rather than as migrant workers, as many women as men arrived, until the infamous "none is too many" policy of the late 1930s was implemented. The anti-Semitism they encountered in Canada was both everyday and structural, but did not necessarily permeate social structures in the same form that racism did for people of colour. For example, while 1930s Toronto parks still posted "No Jews and No Negroes" signs, Jewish migrant families were able to come to make a life here, whereas South Asian and Chinese men and women wishing to migrate in this same period were actively prevented from doing so. That is, the presence of Jews was not welcomed in many ways, yet they were not seen to threaten the whiteness of the Canadian nation-state.

In an anti-Semitic climate, workers were often forced to make choices between class alliances and those of culture and/or religion. Even with the strength and support of Jewish unions, this was complicated, given that many Jewish garment workers had Jewish bosses. Cross-class alliances with the boss often alleviated the closely integrated class-exploitation and ethnic discrimination that Jewish workers experienced. It was hard to get access to "better paying blue collar jobs"[81] outside the garment industry. An opposite dynamic was an active anti-Semitic antagonism by Canadian capitalists towards Jewish workers: their well-developed class consciousness and organization were seen as such a threat that the ruling class often fanned the flames of non-Jewish, working-class, anti-Semitism to undermine the development of broader working-class alliances. The fact that unions were divided into Jewish and non-Jewish locals is a reflection of the structural anti-Semitism of the time, not just of skill and language differences. Yet, structural anti-Semitism in Canada largely faded away after World War Two, likely due to the horror and guilt over having left Jews to their fate in the Holocaust. Perversely, this "helped" Jews move from an "off-white" status to the whiteness they experience today.[82]

The complex interconnected workings of racism, sexism and class exploitation can be seen in other dynamics of waged work at this time. The cultivation of the racialized sexist ideology of white men as bread-winners and white women as fragile and in need of protection clashed with the reality that many white women were working. And the ideology kept their wages low. However, in order to keep white women from abject poverty, women of colour and Aboriginal women got the lowest paying, worst jobs going. During the depression of the 1930s, Black families "survived on the wages of women working in service and of men work-ing as porters on the railroad and in general labour."[83] In fact, up until World War Two, at least 80% of Black women in Canadian cities worked in domestic service. Black women also worked on farms and in the home. This was true even at the time of the Second World War when it was by and large white women who took over white men's jobs. However, the war did release some Black women from domestic service by giving them access to factory and office work. Even with terrible wages and conditions, "the industrial wage ... [was] ... a boon to Black women and the Black community as a whole — despite the laissez-faire racism on the job in the war plants and other industries."[84] Further, upon entering the industrial workforce in World War Two, "Black women felt freer at least to argue against racism on equal footing with the white women they encountered during the war, an increased militancy which led women to get involved with union and other forms of organizing."[85]

After World War Two, although the material conditions of many workers improved with the "boom," immigration policy was "driven by a paranoid, anti-Communist, cold war stance"[86] as well as new labour market needs in this "new phase of capitalist accumulation."[87] After the war, women workers were pushed back into their "traditional" occupations despite huge labour shortages in industry, agriculture and domestic service that led to recruitment of eastern and southern European workers as both free and indentured labour.[88] But the state's desire to maintain the white, Anglo-Saxon imbalance that had been carefully constructed by Confederation meant that more migrants still came from the UK than from anywhere else between 1945 and 1950.

Because of the ongoing labour needs, in the 1950s single Caribbean women came to Canada under household workers permits[89] as part of the "Caribbean Domestic Worker Scheme" implemented by the Canadian government, "when by 1949 the importation of European servants failed to make up the shortage" of domestic workers[90] demanded by private organizations and middle-class citizens. The first known support group for domestic workers in Ontario was around 1958 when Caribbean women met at the Toronto YWCA Caribbean Club on Thursday evenings, the "maids day out."[91] In the 1940s and 50s, the Brotherhood of Sleeping Car Porters, the Negro Citizen's Association of Toronto and others in southwestern Ontario "fought segregation in housing, accommodation, and employment, as well as racist immigration laws."[92] Partly as a result of this organizing work, in 1962 there was an increase in immigration from the Caribbean.

Expanding and continuing the trend of migrant exploitation, in 1973 the federal government started the Non-Immigrant Employment Authorization Program (NIEAP). Within the various programs that continue to fall under this, migrant workers are not permanent residents, they cannot change the terms of their temporary work visas without state permission, and their rights are few, at best. Migrant workers, mainly from the south, come to do the lowest paying, often unsafe jobs. For example, by 1987 women made up 80% of domestic workers in Canada as a whole, 95% of whom were migrants.[93] Further, when we look at migration as a whole, while in 1973 57% of people migrating as workers got permanent resident status, by 1993 only 30% did. This is in sharp contrast to the fast-tracking of permanent residency applications for anyone with enough money to buy their way into the country.

As the NIEAP was expanding, the state had to balance the needs of capital within the intensified racist social climate it had led the way in creating and maintaining. As a result, the state simultaneously allowed entry to more migrants of colour while "increasing the deportation powers of immigration officials as well as setting up [in 1976] a commission on immigration which heard views from Canadians across the country ... [that were] ... significantly racist and exclusionist."[94]

Many Filipinas and other women of colour from the political South migrate under the 'Live-In Caregiver Program' started in 1992. The federal Seasonal Agricultural Workers Program (SAWP) first initiated in the late '60s that brings some 20,000 workers from the Caribbean and Mexico into Canada each year is another example of state-legislated and -regulated different rights based on citizenship and country of origin. While these workers, some of whom are here the majority of the year, sometimes for decades, pay taxes, Employment Insurance and Canada Pension Plan premiums, they are rarely allowed to see one dime of those benefits, they do not have access to the most basic employment standards, and almost never become permanent residents because their time working here does not count towards supporting such an application.[95] Looking at all this, it is easy to see how the federal government has used these kinds of programs to shift immigration policy "towards an increasing reliance upon unfree, migrant labour."[96]

Women who migrate under the immigration law's "family class" definition — which, besides being a migrant worker, is the only real option for most immigrant women of colour — have their lives structured by a state that gives them no rights to subsidized housing, federal language programs or social assistance. It privatizes their existence, as they are supposedly staying at home and taking care of children. This is so prevalent that in 1986, 43% of immigrant women did not know English or

French. In cases of abuse, many women legitimately fear that accessing support services will jeopardize their immigration status.[97]

As we see, "while European-born immigrants represented 90 percent of those who arrived before 1961, they accounted for only 25 percent of those arriving between 1981 and 1991."[98] Sharp shortages in skilled workers again in the early 1960s lead to a liberalizing of immigration policy, replacing in 1967 the most overtly racist components that ranked potential immigrants and set out who was "preferred" with the more implicitly discriminatory points system that continues to tie migration to labour needs. With this we see the Canadian state's attempts to mask institutional racism with apparently non-racist discourse and policy, as it pretends that everyone has equal access because everyone is in equal conditions. This can also be seen as the "increasing commodification of immigrants,"[99] whereby human lives become only as valuable as the services they can provide or the goods they can make. Immigration law has been amended frequently since 1967, such that the fifty points required in 1967 had been raised to seventy in 1992 and, while over the ten years that followed, there were federal politicians' efforts to increase it to as high as eighty, it currently sits at sixty-seven. A head tax of $975 was added in the early 1990s.

Within the points system-based migration, most women able to migrate within the "independent class" are highly educated yet can only get work cleaning and serving because of the multiple racist obstacles in their way. Immigrant and other women of colour are also overrepresented in low-paid factory work. In 1986, "7% of all employed Canadian women ... worked in product fabricating or processing/machining occupations," while the rate was 41% for Southeast Asian Canadian women.[100] These are just more examples of "the direct connection between the lower value of the labour of women in general all over the world, and non-white women in particular, and the profit margins" of big business.[101]

This is particularly significant when we try to ground global phenomena such as "deregulation," "privatization" and "restructuring" in peoples' lives. For example, in Canada, while full-time jobs shrunk by 10% (30% in manufacturing alone) between 1985 and 1995, between 1975 and 1993 there was a 120% increase in part-time jobs, mainly in food, retail and other services.[102] And we know who is doing a disproportionate share of this low-paid, precarious work: women of colour. This is not to say that white working-class folks' labour is not also exploited for profit or that many white people don't live in poverty. It is to say that racism (and sexism) deepen the exploitation of workers of colour. For example, both white and non-white women work as nurses, but Black women tend to get the most physically demanding work.[103] But, despite this burden, women of colour have organized themselves.

There were many organizations and groups of women of colour before the state set up and funded agencies. In fact, the state's involvement in immigrant women's issues was as a result of the increased migration in the 1970s of non-white people, the international revolutionary movements, the local anti-racist, anti-colonialist and civil rights struggles and the women's movement. Many non-white people in Canada have long been involved in organizing around police violence and racism in the education system.[104] Feminist movements themselves arose out of a combination of anti-poverty, pro-choice and anti-racist struggles. And although white women by and large were not grappling with the challenge of anti-racist feminism, in many cases, both white and non-white "lesbians were the backbone of much of multiracial institution building in the 1970s and 1980s."[105] All these factors came together "to make Native, Black, South-East Asian and South Asian women a constituency to be recognized."[106] As a result, the benefits that have come from multiculturalism were achieved through struggle; they did not come as a gift. Further, even the biological origin definition of racism was changed by such on the ground anti-racist resistance so that we came to understand it as not just beliefs but "all actions, individual and institutional" that sustained or increased the subjugation of non-white people.[107]

In just 1985, as a result of Aboriginal women's organizing, one of the most devastating racist sexist provisions of the 1876 Indian Act was changed so that Native women would no longer lose their legal Aboriginal status if they married non-Native men. This is just one example of how different forms of repression call for different strategies in response.

As we have seen with the many examples above, historically as today, racism takes different forms when we analyze it in relation to other power relations. For another example, sexism has treated most women at one time or another as "breeders," so that motherhood gets glorified or ignored for different reasons of social control. In Canada, this has meant that, while "Anglo-Saxon women were constructed to be mothers of the nation, South-Asian Canadian women were constructed as mothers of ethnic communities."[108] And, women of colour continue to be workers first. One thing this means is the continuing state-sanctioned separation of migrant women of colour from their children. It is these women's work that often allows some white women to raise their wages and ladder-climb, effectively "exercising class and citizenship privilege" to lessen the burden of sexism.[109] And so we see another effective contradiction: the Third World woman "pitied as passive, dismissed as tradition bound," yet, when capitalism's need for labour requires it, the same woman becomes "the world's cheapest source of labour," often working the hardest, longest hours.[110]

This integration of different forms of oppressive power relations with class exploitation can also been seen in two contrasting cases of Chinese migrants to British Columbia. Kathryne Mitchell reviews the late 1980s' purchase of a number of Vancouver condominiums by Hong Kong-based ruling-class people and the Canadian state's role in easing the burden of racism to challenge the mainly white middle- and working-class local outcry against these purchases.[111] The basis of local concern seems to have been a contradictory mix of a legitimate wish for affordable housing in the area rather than more private, expensive homes, and a racism-fuelled demonstration of anxiety over "individual and national identity as well as a concern about urban change." As such, the usual cross-class alliance based on white supremacy failed to meet ruling-class objectives in this case: the priority was to smooth the way for ruling-class purchase of real estate so the BC government took the role of decrying racism to discredit Vancouver protesters. If one buys the race-relations model of eradicating discrimination, this could appear as a positive step forward on the part of the state in getting rid of racism rather than an example of how, when racism gets in the way of "the social networks necessary for the integration of international capitalisms," it has to be selectively managed.[112]

To grasp this, one need only contrast this case with the one of Chinese migrants who arrived in Vancouver by boat in 1999, without money to invest but with a legitimate need and desire for refuge. The Canadian state's response was to fan the flames of white Canadians' everyday racism to buttress structural forms of racist exclusion in the face of progressive demands for asylum for the migrants. Calling the people "illegal" and focussing on the fact that they were "smuggled" in, and invoking the usual kinds of images and ideas about who has a right to be here, a legitimate claim to safety and to share in "our" national identity, the state played the opposite—and more well known—role than that of ten years before. These migrants' applications for refugee status were fast-tracked; indeed, most were deported within a rather short period of time.

Due to ongoing dissent in the face of such racism, it is not strategic for state organizations, nationally and internationally, to completely ignore the existence of that dissent so they do turn their rhetorical attention on occasion to racism. As a result of First Nations' focussing part of their struggle on the international stage, in 2002 the United Nations (UN) Committee on the Elimination of Racial Discrimination criticized the Canadian government for not doing enough to deal with the racism inherent in: 1) the failure to settle land claims; 2) the number of Native deaths in police custody; and 3) the lack of access of Aboriginal people to the legal system. The same report also criticized the state for "ethnic stereotyping" of various immigrants and people of colour as terrorists.[113] Quite an important statement, but what teeth does the UN have to transform the concern into change? As we saw with the UN security council's slow, difficult march to be part of the US-led war on Iraq, the answer seems to be "just about none."

Clearly, ethnic stereotyping barely describes what is happening in Canada today. In June 2002, the Immigrant and Refugee Protection Act came into law with the passing of Bill C-11. It gives immigration officials more power to detain immigrants and refugees as well as more powers to decide refugee claims are ineligible. The interaction of this law with Bill C-36, the Anti-Terrorism legislation, and the Safe Third Country agreement between the US and Canada, is nothing short of frightening. Terrorism is itself left undefined in C-36, C-11 allows inadmissibility of claims and detention on the basis of ill-defined "security risks," and refugee claimants coming to Canada via the US can and will be turned back.[114] And it does not stop there. Bill C-18, The Citizenship of Canada Act, would have created a two-tier citizenship by allowing the state to deny, revoke or annul citizenship of non-Canadian-born people. This would have been possible "without consultation, disclosure of evidence, independent review or the opportunity to appeal the decision."[115]

All these measures amount to nothing short of a dangerous intensification of legal racism. The social and political space for these vile laws has been opened by the hysteria of the so-called war on terrorism, whipped up by imperialism to justify its expanded control, by any means necessary, of natural resources and land, wealth, people's rights to movement and even to their very existence.

Still today, even in a society heavily promoted by the ruling class as open for multicultural business,[116] it is whiteness that is the foundation of whatever we understand as "Englishness, Frenchness and finally Europeanness" of Canada, and "whiteness extends into moral qualities of masculinity, possessive individualism and an ideology of capital and the market" as well as a hostility to "others."[117]

Divide and Rule Continues: Multiculturalism Policy and Practice

> When you are black-skinned, it often matters little if the person refusing to rent to you is Polish-, Anglo-, or Italian-Canadian. The result is the same. And multiculturalism, as we presently know it, has no answers to these or other problems such as the confrontation between the police forces in urban areas like Toronto and Montréal and the African-Canadian communities that live there.[118]

Multiculturalism policy and practice has been a "highly problematic and contradictory"[119] tool that, in comparison with other Western countries, is uniquely applied in Canada. As a term, it is best when used to describe the population mix in Canada, "which is characterized by a heterogenous ethnic composition, the racial complexity of which has multiplied as a result of increased immigration from non-European source countries since the 1970s."[120] In fact, by 1987, 70% of immigrants had such origins.[121]

The official state policy was a result of three factors, more or less in the following order of significance: the need to forge a new national identity in a fragmented, geographically dispersed nation-state; the ruling-class challenge of dealing with Quebec nationalism; and the need to contain anti-racist struggles by addressing the impact of increasing migration of non-white people.

The policy has resulted in some practical benefits and relief. For example, there is a somewhat better social climate of "tolerance" of people of colour in Canada than in some other Western nations. In contrast to Canada, France has a determined universalist, secularist approach to civic life that flies in the face of often intense racism from a far right much more significant in size than Canada's.[122] One could also speculate that this greater white Canadian "tolerance" of people of colour has geographic and demographic roots as well. There is no third-world country bordering Canada so the state can look much friendlier in its general treatment of (for example) Mexican visitors and migrants as it quietly supports the US doing its dirty work. And, demographically, Canada-wide migrants of colour still remain a relatively small percentage and a relatively small population, in contrast with geographically smaller, more populated western European nations.

As well, although on the decline, some amounts of funding have been available here to some immigrants with the right papers for official language training. By and large, however, the policy has had a significant negative impact on organizing around anti-racist demands by converting racism into race relations. This is not an accident; on the contrary, it fits into an overall nation-state policy of putting white Canada first, controlling non-white people and making sure that some of the insiders (immigrants and other people of colour) maintain their outsider status.

This new shift in racism-based social control was developed in the 1970s, at a time when the post-war boom was forgotten in the wake of an economic crisis that created a need for lower and lower waged workers, which meant more migrants of colour. Although opposed by the right and not originally intended to have only this function, Canadian multicultural social policy has ended up supporting neo-liberal political economic policy in propelling the rightward direction of our society in the last few decades. The fragmenting and marginalizing consequences of multicultural policy delivery fit well with the rolling back of social programs and with "an aggressive market-oriented economic doctrine and highly individualistic social philosophy."[123]

The Quebecois nationalism that started to flourish in the early '60s — which, at the time, had both moderate and militantly radical forms—was an important social force in the 1971 passing of the Multiculturalism Act:

> The adoption of official bilingualism in 1969 and then multiculturalism in 1971 was a calculated move aimed at compromising the demands of French Canadians and the aspirations of those not of British or French origin ... [as] ... it promoted an ideological claim of cultural choice for all Canadians to counteract the demand of special status underlining Quebec's separatist sentiments.[124]

Multiculturalism therefore became the ideological glue in the recent history of the construction of the Canadian capitalist nation-state as it made the necessary move from a white settler colony to a liberal democracy.

Often multiculturalism is expressed in the form of a kind of pluralism that says individuals can make "personal cultural choices" to keep their "personal cultural life," including language, but only in the private sphere because the publicly funded and supported life is to be "Canadian" and the languages that go along with this are only English or French. The fact that most of us considered to be of real Anglo-Saxon British or French origin are white, and that non-French or non-Anglos are in the majority disappears as we now all apparently have these individual cultural options from which to chose.[125]

And so the eradication of racism and the fight for true equality disappear into the void of this narrow and opportunistic idea of culture that shifts between two contradictory poles. On the one hand, people of colour are subjected to frozen-in-time ideas of tradition and culture that range from romantic to dangerous: all Aboriginal people know how to survive in the bush and are very spiritual; most Black men are Jamaican and have a pre-disposition to crime and pursuing white women; and all Arabs are suspects or sympathizers of terrorism. At the other pole is an anti-essentialist notion that transforms particular cultural practices for everyone's entertainment and commodification. For example, white folks strip dreadlocks of political significance by wearing them, and sweat lodges become another deep experience for non-Aboriginals at expensive weekend retreats.

Instead of dealing with racism, multiculturalism therefore explains differences in behaviour and attitudes to try to get us all to adapt to and then celebrate our differences through potlucks and parades. This adaptation is deemed necessary because it is supposedly the differences rather than institutionalized inequality that create conflict.[126] While non-white people become hyper-ethnicized, we white folks remain the de-ethnicized models of Canadian-ness. Just how "different" non-white people are is "measured or constructed in terms of distance from civilizing European cultures."[127] It "has also produced a peculiar brand of "Canadian racism" described by many as 'polite,' 'subtle,' 'systemic,' and even 'democratic.'"[128] What this also means is that people of colour are supposed to adapt to racism and white people are apparently removed of our responsibility for it.

The rising demands of people of colour, which the state so wished to compromise on, to contain and control through multicultural policy, are a fundamental threat to elites. Of particular concern have been those struggles of immigrant women of colour. Who would do all those underpaid, at times unsafe, nanny jobs if migrant women workers won rights to permanent residency and so had a few more options in their work conditions as well as more freedom to further organize for higher wages and better jobs? Instead, the state believes, it's better to put in place some reforms such as community-specific social programs.[129] The social control goal has been met with the support of some segments of the target communities. Criticisms of the limited symbolic nature came from the left and Aboriginal people generally saw multicultural policy as doing nothing to advance their struggle for self-determination, but some leaders of particular communities of colour (depending upon their political and/or class position) got the official state recognition that they sought and so got behind the program.

Even while it has served the state well, nonetheless the hostility of the elites and dominant society toward multicultural policy started in the 1980s with the start of large-scale contraction in manufacturing industries, deregulation, erosion of the welfare state and the negotiation of "free" trade agreements. Due to the tight link between multiculturalism and immigration, socially and economically, white hostility to the former meant an equal hostility to non-white migration from the South. Yet, at the same time, the federal government started to link its multicultural policy with business development. While both Tories and Liberals have done this now, it was Brian Mulroney who initiated the "Multiculturalism Means Business" conference in 1986. So we see once again how the state must juggle increasing racist contradictions: on one hand, through middle- and upper-class immigrants, "we, as a nation need to grasp the opportunity afforded to us by our multicultural identity, to cement our prosperity."[130] On the other hand, even as more workers are needed to do increasingly precarious, lower-waged jobs, the ruling class blames those same migrants for somehow stealing "our" higher wage jobs that are being lost in the wake of neo-liberalism.

In 1993 the whole multicultural bureaucracy was "abruptly submerged" into the Heritage Department[131] and by 1996, the need for intense state multicultural policy promotion and funding was at an end because it had already become an integral feature of "our" national identity. Neo-liberalism's ongoing need for deeper and deeper social program cuts dovetailed with this to produce the "Strategic Evaluation of Multicultural Programs." In 1997, the federal Liberals put forward a new "program" with three goals: "identity, participation and justice."[132] The ideological piece of the neo-liberal shift had now been further developed: your identity is your private matter, you must volunteer to meet any needs that result from that and, as a result, you will reach another symbolic place of social justice. This shift eventually resulted in a move from the promotion of identity labels (for example, South Asian-, Carib-bean-, et cetera, Canadians) to the language of "special interest groups" competing for shrinking pots of funds. Along with this shift came what Bannerji calls an "ethnicization of politics, shifting (the) focus from unemployment due to high profit margins, or flight of capital, to 'prob-lems' presented by immigrants' own culture and tradition."[133] To ad-dress the "cultural conflicts" that arise from such "problems," diversity workshops now pepper the landscape of both non-profit and corporate organizations. At best, white folks are signed up at the first whiff of a complaint of racism, often coded and diluted by white managers as "inappropriate behaviour."[134]

One on-the-ground economic impact of all this for immigrants of colour can be a community-based isolation. As multiculturalism has created a mask for "community" as all things traditional and good, class distinctions within various communities are apparently erased. For example, non-white elites of a particular language group and/or country of origin, perhaps marginalized by racism within capitalism, nonetheless have the means to set up their own industries and service-based businesses. One such business becoming more common to workers generally, as a result of neo-liberal attacks on workers' job security, wages and conditions, is the "temporary agency," which supplies workers on a short-term basis to companies who then save money and time on hiring employees directly. Working-class immigrants excluded by racism and sexism from a chance at getting the higher waged, more secure jobs that still exist in the labour market as a whole — an exclusion often coded as "lack of Canadian experience" — and/or without English or French language skills often end up in the most underpaid, insecure and unsafe types of employment. The Workers' Action Centre in Toronto works with many Sri Lankan-Canadian women working for Sri Lankan-Canadian temp agency employers. Reporting on this kind of phenomenon in Los Angeles, Hoon Lee suggests that "the hidden side of the Korean success story was that it relied in large part on the exploitation of cheap Korean immigrant labor."[135]

And so now we have a climate in this democratic, diverse society of "ours" in which a child of colour yelling "trick or treat" too loudly for a white neighbour's taste can be confidently screamed back at to be quiet because he's "acting like a terrorist."[136] We have increasing deportations of refugee claimants to dangerous political climates in their countries of origin as well as limitations on who can legitimately make a refugee claim depending on how they managed, against all odds, to get themselves to our kind and gentle nation. We are living in a climate of veritable hysteria about "our" safety and security, about protecting "ourselves" from dark, sinister threats. Despite initial state attempts to stem a potential tide of organizing by managing the intensified, on-the-street, everyday racism after the September 11, 2001 attacks on the US, the centuries of white rule in Canada have laid a foundation so firm that it can only be removed with serious social transformation.

Within this historically systemic racism, we can see the complex and different locations of white and non-white people today in Canada. But it is not so easy to apply what we know because of that persistent remorse-based anti-racism, the often silent complicity of whites with racism and its benefits, and because there are limits to acting based on personal responsibility alone: without the broader social conditions for effective organizing, effective anti-racism work is tough to do.

It is useful now to ask questions about what most white activists and unionists are learning about anti-racism and how we are applying it to effect real change. We will then be able to outline some organizing principles as a foundation for improving our community and union anti-racist work.

4

Where White Activists And Unionists Learn About Anti-Racism

Introduction

From its beginnings as a participatory, research for action, project in the year 2000 with two staff and good community connections, Toronto Organizing for Fair Employment (TOFFE) has now morphed into the bigger and more dynamic Workers' Action Centre (WAC). WAC now has seven staff, forty to fifty active members, and 2000 workers in their database, all representative of the multiracial character of the majority of low-waged workers living in Toronto. Although no one at WAC would say their work has been easy, their efforts do represent the kind of anti-racist organizing that can be a solid foundation of real social change.

This chapter will look in more detail at WAC and other hopeful models of community-based anti-racist organizing. We will also look at a variety of other community agencies, activist groups, unions and academia, to explore the variety of approaches to and ideas about anti-racism out there. This is important because what we do is deeply connected to what we think about what we do, whether we are conscious of it or not. As such, this chapter will make the links between the sources of white activists' anti-racist learning, the ideas that we have about anti-racism, and the activities we find ourselves involved in. By making these links we can develop a useful critique of white anti-racism that will help point the way forward to seeking out, participating in and developing solid community-based, anti-racist projects.

This chapter is divided into two major sections: the first is a thematic analysis of what we learn from various anti-racist activities and teaching available to us; the second is an overview of the sources of our learning. The first section will give us insight into the often-unconscious ideological dilemmas created in us by what we learn in our community groups, unions, and university or college courses. By looking at this we can start to grapple with why what we often learn is not effective. Then, in the second section, we can review concrete examples of just where these ideas are coming from.

From Theory to Practice and Back Again:
The Ideas Behind Anti-Racist Activity and Education

We can learn quite different things about racism and anti-racism, depending on where we are connected in our community activism and/or if we are unionized workers who have access to some kind of training. It is useful to look these sources of information through the following themes: agency and structure; culture, difference, and identity; social relations; understanding whiteness for understanding white supremacy; and organizing for change.

Agency and Structure

In political terms, we can think of "agency" as the ability of exploited and oppressed people to use what they know and understand from their own experience to resist and struggle. Although maybe not so frequently thought of as part of agency, I would also include in the definition what we do individually and collectively that results in our benefitting from the oppression of others as a result of our own conscious or unconscious actions, and how these actions interact with structures of domination. Presently, there are many such structures intertwined with the power of business and the state. But, when it comes to understanding racism, much of what white leftists come in contact with fails to show the interrelationship of such a full definition of agency with structural forces, both in terms of oppression and exploitation, and in terms of how we fight them.

Typically, many parts of the far left do not like to think of the working class as having any agency beyond that of resisting capital and they like to think of the expression of structural forces solely as a function of what the ruling class does to workers. For example, Theodore Allen, a prominent theorist in the area of whiteness studies, questions why white workers in the late nineteenth century would have identified themselves as white when they could have identified themselves as workers and made class alliances against racism and exploitation together.[1] However, this is not so puzzling if we consider both the weakness of working class collectivity on the whole and the powerful forces that ensured that white workers would materially and socially benefit from a racist, cross-class alliance instead: they were given access to or the hope of access to privilege and the potential to become the entitled. It was real, tangible benefit that was and is part of these initiatives for social control, not just ideas that created the racialized environment before and after white workers fully came into their white supremacy. This is not to say that it is natural for people to make self-interested and oppressive choices over ones of solidarity: it is to say that both those choices are not made in a vacuum;

they are made in the historically specific circumstances in which the way ruling class power shapes class struggle can leave little room to do the right thing. It was exactly this "system of social control"[2] that operated to improve Irish-Americans' position in the white, ethnic hierarchy.

Just as there is an inadequate understanding of why agency is used to do the wrong thing, there is a tendency to let white workers off the hook for our own racism. It is often said by some far left thinkers that white workers use racism to explain why they are exploited and poor in their everyday lives, to make sense of the world around them; that is, how workers use "discourse, categories and stereotypes that are available in the local white culture" to understand their own situation.[3] This white racism in Canada is seen time and time again as Aboriginal people and immigrants of colour are thought to receive unfair special treatment from equity programs. As well, white workers have understood the coincidence of the crises in capitalist production and their own job loss in certain periods, along with the rolling back of the social programs, as the fault of increased migration of non-white people. In effect, "racism helps make sense of economic and social changes."[4] If we end the explanation for white racism here, we are suggesting that the white working class is not involved in generating racist ideas and action, and that we are therefore not responsible for those ideas because those perspectives simply explain our world to us. Leaving it there also builds no connection with the significant social control efforts of elites who are intensely involved in producing and maintaining the ideas that immigrants and beer-drinking welfare recipients are our collective (read, white) problem. White workers often take up these ideas and pass them on as well, even though white folks get thrown into that mix as part of the "white trash" beer-drinking component of the racist and class-biased ruling class diss.

This also points to another related matter. A strong belief in the power of our agency should not cause us to make the mistake of thinking that we all inherently know what is best for us or that we have a full analysis of our circumstances all the time. Bannerji clearly points out how flawed this reasoning is:

> since political subjectivities are articulated within a given political and ideological environment, and self-identities are fraught with contradictory possibilities ... victims and subjects of capital do not automatically become socialists. Misery does not automatically produce communism, and desire for change born of suffering does not spontaneously know 'what is to be done?' to end oppression.[5]

A narrow focus on agency also does not shed any light on why we are not, instead, blaming the ruling class for the damage they are doing. If we are just making sense of the world, why is that in a predominantly racist way? If there is an overt effort by the ruling class operating on both tangible and ideological fronts, why don't we see that and reject it? These questions show how we need to see our agency in its fullness and as part of the workings of structures of domination if we are to appreciate, and hope to realize, the potential of agency at all. There are powerful forces at work to make white workers make cross-class alliances instead of working-class ones.

Another case of lack of attention to the relationship between agency and structure is found in much community-based anti-racism training and in the postmodern ideas about identity, difference and the unmooring of power that partially influence that training. In the best workshops, systems of domination are signalled as the historical and ongoing source of power and privilege, allowing us then to see where we fit with our individual identities into all this. Since racism operates at everyday and structural levels, pulling apart the systems to see where we each fit in is important. But the problem is, once we have pulled them apart, we often don't know what to do next. Systemic power and the individual power of privilege do not get woven together to show how all the experiences of poverty and oppression are integrated into capitalist society. The systems of domination are left in the background, floating there alongside us, as we get lost in our sea of identities.

Culture, Difference and Identity

> The concept of conflicting social pressure and identities is clearly valid. The problem arises ... when all 'identities' ... are treated as if of equal social value .... If this were true ... then racism would not be a problem. If we could choose identities like we choose our clothes every morning, if we could erect social boundaries from a cultural Lego pack, then racial hostility would be no different from disagreements between lovers of Mozart and those who prefer Charlie Parker, or between supporters of different football clubs. In other words there would be no social content to racial differences, simply prejudices borne out of a plurality of tastes and outlooks.[6]

The sources of our multiple identities become blurred. In the honouring of agency, identities are apparently there for the choosing and so can become sources of a neutralized idea of difference and diversity. Power floats by, always changing how it looks and where it happens. One result of this is that white people are let off the hook. In this identity sea we can feel better about privilege—and not even deal with white supremacy—because the whole is so fragmented and too complicated. Our solution is then often two-fold: an idealistic honouring of conventional notions of non-white groups' traditional cultural beliefs and practices, and a collection of identities for ourselves so we can relate to the impact of identities on "others."

In order to understand racism, we then start to understand that we too need an ethnic identity on which to draw. This is often a romantic attachment to a mythical, traditional, Anglo-Saxon past. Once we have our Celtic goddess alongside us, we can bridge the difference gap, because we too have an ethnic identity. Once we are grounded in power-free cultural differences as the source of our understanding and work around racism, we slip away from the fact that it is not a choice to be paid poverty wages for doing the service, care-giving and cleaning work done by a disproportionate number of non-white women; it's not a choice to be refused entry into Canada because your country of origin is Yemen, not the UK; there are no identities self-selected or negotiated when Black women are all too frequently strip-searched at the airport. Aboriginal men freezing in the Saskatchewan rural night are dying because cops have the state power, fuelled by centuries of racism as well as by class bias, to drive them out and drop them there.[7]

Material and social benefits flow from oppression, not from being different. Our collective power is in our resistance to and struggle against oppression, not in the oppression itself, as an over-emphasis on choosing and negotiating identifies would have us believe. As white folks, the power is also in our privilege and how we use it. If taking on a goddess helps us get through life, if reading non-Christian religious texts like the Koran helps us relate to spiritual practices of non-white groups in a way that helps us build relationships, then we should encourage these practices in those of us who find them useful and meaningful. But these are not generally political nor specifically anti-racist practices in and of themselves, and can actually deepen stereotypes.

> It is economic benefits and other social advantages that place a dominant group in its position of domination, rather than any particular lack of understanding of individuals from one group about the culture of the individuals from the other ... often cultural symbols such as language, dress, etc may become points of contention between oppressors and subordinates. However, these areas are more likely the consequence rather than the cause of the inequalities between the two groups.[8]

Turning such nostalgic attachments into anti-racist solutions can easily happen in a context in which we have reduced culture to multiple, fixed "unconscious tradition(s)" rather than "conscious activity,"[9] as a "genetic inheritance"[10] usually rooted in a specific geographic place of origin. As the postmodernists carry out their "project of deconstruction and reconstruction" of culture, they actually "dehistoricize, decontextualize, devalidate and mythologize" their efforts.[11] This fits like a glove with state multiculturalism policy and practice.

Along the same lines, when it comes to what some whiteness studies proponents see as diminishing the power of whiteness through cultural "crossover,"[12] a legitimate question to ask then is, "Where is the line between rip off and respect?" Paul Rubio contends that in order to improve our humanity, we whites learn, take on and enjoy non-white cultural expressions such as music: "White cultural assimilation is not the same thing as political defection from the white race, but it is already a form of political awareness."[13] Salim Washington cautions against taking this much farther, saying that such so-called race traitors are romanticized, because "American music was forever changed (by Black musicians), but the status of black musicians remained the same."[14]

This demonstrates graphically another common problem of our understanding of cultural crossover for anti-racism: when we are not careful, once again we tend to see non-white people through a prism of multiple cultural differences and so try to bridge the gaps merely as consumers and appropriators. We take on what we can mimic, what we can buy or use, in order to fill our own vacuum and, in the process, we assume this is automatically anti-racist. As a result, it is as if we can choose from, take on or compete with an endless supply of "competing interests built on the concept of the free market."[15] In this process the possibilities shrink for questioning whether there is a positive systemic impact on the actual conditions of life for people of colour when white interest shines a spotlight on non-white cultural activity. The result can be deepening appropriation instead of increased support on the road to liberation.

This is not meant to caricature white folks' legitimate connection with and appreciation for non-Anglo-Saxon-origin music, art and literature. And it is fair to say that the US context is more extreme than the

Canadian context in terms of the crossover issue. The pro-multicultural environment of Canadian society of the last number of decades has made "learning about the others" a positive, desirable and mainstreamed phenomenon. So, it is not all bad. As culture has become narrowed and hyper-commodified within the political economy, white exposure to, and interest in, African drumming, salsa and merengue dancing, and novels by South Asian-Canadian writers are all positive steps in an anti-racist direction. But is the next step simply feeling more comfortable with ourselves for having improved "race relations" and enriched our lives, or is it taking social risks by denouncing white supremacy and racism and fighting it in our workplaces and neighbourhoods?

The idea that something called "culture" is the source of either op-pression or liberation is complicated and problematic. It is true that "when race is discussed, an aspect/dimension least raised is whiteness and white privilege. An examination of the everyday, common-sense knowledge and practice of racism reveals the ascription of race to 'oth-ers' but not to the dominant group."[16] Because it is such a problematic concept, in this process of assigning or even taking on "race," the use of the term "race" often becomes replaced by the term "culture." But when that happens, whiteness and the idea that white supremacy is based on a "culture" of whiteness mask the social relations looked at above. At the same time, breaking whites down into German-Canadians, Scottish-Canadians and so on, attaching these original identities, is not the answer because it "highlights cultural heritage ... (and so) ... denies whiteness as a phenomenon worth scrutinizing and with it, racism."[17] Again, we see that the pursuit of "our own" cultural identity is not necessarily anti-racist activity.

For example, I can be "me" quite easily in public: I'm a straight, Ca-nadian-born WASP who is adequately employed to meet my basic needs. This apparent identity, the heritage behind it, is not erased from public space. On the contrary, it is front and centre. I am afforded a freedom of movement, self-definition and self-expression because of it. But if I do not see these power relations and instead focus on the cultural component, what could that mean? If I step forward and proudly proclaim Irish Protestant working-class roots, how does that resist racism? What does that do to make visible my friends and neighbours? The answer is, quite simply, nothing at all. As well, the very idea that a person can "give up" whiteness as an identity is troubling. We can challenge it, we can "use it for the forces of good," but to promote this without a collective, multiracial program for change denies the systemic nature and force of racism.

It is still important to appreciate fluidity and choice. In the blinding whiteness that controls our society—who gets what jobs, who is running the governments and business, who controls the media—the lives of people of colour are generally erased, made invisible, except when it comes to crime, terrorism or deportations. In such a climate, publicly expressing and/or acknowledging different aspects of one's identity can cause further marginalization, and can be downright dangerous. Affirmations of identity can be acts of real resistance to the compartmentalization of racism. Finding and creating those social spaces in which someone can define and celebrate their Africanness, their Jewishness and/or their lesbianness is to defy domination. In such a context, cultural reclaiming, expression of a national, cultural and/or sexual identity by people of colour, can be key to forcing silenced voices and invisibility onto the broad Canadian public space. So, while it is not inherently transformational, this cultural and other identity affirmation is often about survival and, by association, anti-racist.

Social Relations and Integrated Analysis

The social relations of racism, sexism and class-based exploitation, and the power inherent in these, can be lost when "being different" becomes distanced from systemic exploitation and oppression.[18] Much of what we learn about anti-racism lacks an analysis of power that is historical and interconnected, and that talks about agency and structure at the same time. Such an understanding should see that power is "not a thing—it is a complex field of relationships, including coercive ones, and the ability to produce ideas" that have influence.[19]

Yet, on the one hand, we have postmodernism, in which society becomes an "accidental interaction between individuals,"[20] with our subjective experience of life and our ever-shifting power bases cut out of social experience as a whole. From postmodern ideas, we understand that power is a moving target, which makes coordinated strategies of resistance useless: "in an era of global capitalism, the heralding of subject positions 'at the margins' too often neglects the actual marginalization of subjects."[21] As well, postmodernism's focus on discourse and language as if they were representative of the wholeness of our day-to-day lives has the effect of pushing our material realities into the background or of ignoring them altogether.[22]

On the other hand, we have some far leftists' oversimplified structural explanations that reduce all forms of oppression to one-dimensional tools of capitalism's working-class exploitation. This can make anti-racist struggle seem secondary, look like it's outside the economic context of class conflict. That is, "it reduces the context of black struggle to issue-specific anti-racist campaigns that seek to change specific policies ... and ... homogenizes black actors."[23]

In between these poles we have those whiteness theorists who forget about non-white people because of whiteness's often excessive focus on white folks. As Barbara Fields says, "whereas exploring how European immigrants became white is all the rage, no one deems it pertinent to such exploration to ask how African and Afro-Caribbeans became black."[24] We also have some really good anti-racist education and action that unfortunately often resist naming or centring capitalism as the global framework within which we are struggling and shaping our day-to-day lives "as individuals, as members of social classes and as part of defined communities."[25]

Thinking of oppression and exploitation in terms of social relations allows us to understand universal projects — whether it is imperialism's or ours — through the combination of various people's own experiences of domination as well as the collective social origins of these. Such an approach shows us that "there is a direct connection between the lower value of the labour of women in general all over the world, and the labour of non-white women in particular, and the profit margin."[26] Sexism and racism are crucial to the workings, movements and profit margins of multinational corporations. Such an understanding allows us to begin to appreciate how women of colour consciously experience their race, class and sex at the same time; their personal experience and knowledge are key to collective struggle. This, then, is the basis for an integrated analysis for action.

In this context we can understand the intensification, the growing virulence of both everyday and structural anti-Arab and -West Asian racism in the last few decades as connected to imperialist expansion in the Middle East. And, as we discussed in the previous chapter, nation-building also forms a part of this reality as nationalism — even the supposedly watered-down Canadian kind — and racism "are not independent and autonomous forces but are generated and reproduced within a complex interplay of historically constituted economic and power relations."[27]

Understanding Whiteness for Understanding White Supremacy

One area of whiteness study that looks at the development of whiteness and white supremacy traces this history of social construction in the context of the development of capitalism; that is, with the focus on how white supremacy and privilege are handed out to, and accepted by, the working class. This area of whiteness study is most helpful in shedding light on aspects of the historical development of white supremacy in the white working class. Yet parts of the foundation do not sit firmly. To describe the phenomenon of white non-Anglo Saxons as "becoming white" blurs the distinction between the white and non-white experience of being racialized in both Canada and the US.[28] This is not to advocate for a hierarchy of racial oppression or for a competition in misery. It is also not to deny, for example, the centuries of oppression that Irish Catholics have experienced at the hands of England. Rather, the very fact that Irish-Catholic workers knew oppression so well would make us think that their common cause with African Americans would have been self-evident for them. This fact shows how powerful and complex historical circumstances come together to affect our agency. Therefore, we need to be accurate about the quality and enduring nature of oppression that social groups face and struggle with to really understand our historical place in it and our role in fighting it today.

As such, I think it would be more accurate to say that Irish-Catholic workers in the US, and eastern and southern Europeans both north and south of the US-Canada border, did not so much "become white" as experience a flattening of the ethnic hierarchy within white privilege and supremacy. While Italian- and Ukrainian-Canadians did experience ethnically based discrimination that deepened their class exploitation, their conditions did not rival those of non-white workers. For one thing, they were allowed to migrate, whereas non-white workers faced severe restrictions to migration to the point of impossibility in most cases. As well, they were never legally considered "not white." There were articles of the US Constitution and Supreme Court decisions that explicitly delineated white people vs. non-white people, based on skin colour. Granting citizenship rights on that basis shows that while Irish Catholics were ethnically oppressed, they were more than likely always white in terms of formal political rights. Further, there was no biological category for European immigrants "on the basis of the one-drop-of-blood or any-known-ancestry rule that applies to African-Americans."[29]

The ethnic discrimination towards white non-Anglos, while rooted in a history of British empire building, could be said to have been more practical — for more purely economic reasons — rather than both practical and ideological. As we have seen, the practical and the ideological are intricately linked. However, the long history and continuity of the existence of racism — in its ever-changing forms — make racism in Canada more enduring and extensive than what is solely required by the ruling class for their labour requirements. Aboriginal people and non-white people who migrated to escape slavery or came as paid workers have not been offered the historical circumstances to be included in the "White man's country" definition, nor to be free of the brutality of racism. There is nowhere to go in the political West for that. In the historic hierarchy of desirable versus undesirable immigrants, white migrants were moved up to the privileged rungs of desirability quickly because they were "more apt to assimilate to British culture than other 'undesirable' immigrants."[30] Even when labour shortages required lifting restrictions on non-white migration, there was no eventual sea-change of non-white to white, because skin-privileged-based racism and the white supremacy that is the basis of it are fundamental to the organization of Canadian society and economy. In fact, in the 1930s, British Columbia had a different minimum wage for white and non-white workers in the lumber industry: the state put this policy in place to recruit more white workers.[31] The ruling class was willing to pay more money, to actually cut into their business profits, because of (in this case, anti-Asian) racism.

By the late nineteenth and early twentieth centuries, Canada had such a deep and brutal legacy of racism already integrated into the social structure that there was every possibility of a flattening of the ethnic hierarchy for all whites. This was, in fact, realized when capitalist development bloomed after World War Two and real-life conditions vastly improved for many working-class whites. The same legacy also allowed for an ongoing, firmly rooted white supremacy/non-white oppression, despite the gradual improvement of social conditions for relatively few non-white workers.

Another issue in terms of radical whiteness politics and white supremacy is connected with the journal *Race Traitor*. Its editors dismiss all anti-racists as liberals, which is deeply problematic. To summarily dismiss the array of non-white peoples' anti-racist activism is nothing short of a form of white supremacy in itself. Whiteness cannot be championed in any form, even if the goal is abolition. Taking a back seat, not being so self-aggrandizing, is a big part of white anti-racist work. "While much attention is paid to how whites can divest themselves of racial prejudices and engage in significant anti-racist work, the struggles of people of colour remain in the shadows."[32]

Organizing for Change

As organizers fighting for social transformation, a key question for us is, how are we applying anti-racism for change? Partly because of the gaps in what we learn, our anti-racist practice needs serious work. There's also a challenge in translating ideas to action: actively taking risks to confront racism in our day-to-day lives is much more difficult than taking intellectual ones.

It is important to say that white activists in multiracial groups do at times have a good anti-racist practice, demonstrating a degree of effectiveness at assuming enough responsibility to learn how to take direction. We really do get it sometimes. What is interesting to pursue as well is the issue of white anti-racists using those good politics to go further and being that political bridge between communities of colour and areas of white-dominated society that are not touched by those politics. As Sarita Ahooja put it, "We need organized white folks taking on other white folks."[33] When useful white anti-racists are not working in those multiracial milieux, are we taking on the white-dominated union executive? Are we challenging the fact that our workplaces are a white majority? What are we doing with other whites? Do we even think of racism when people of colour are not around and there are no everyday racist remarks to challenge?[34] At the end of the day, we need not just create the space for non-status migrants' voices to challenge racism; we need to be engaged in the fight against white supremacy in mainstream society as well. At the same time, we are all affected by the difficult social conditions we face today, whether we are white or activists of colour. So, building a group of anti-racist "organized white folks" faces many of the broad challenges we have been discussing, as does building an anti-racist movement as a whole.

In the fall of 2001, with the impending attacks on Afghanistan and the actual targeting of migrants in Canada, a number of anti-racist, anti-war groups were organized with the name the Coalition Against War and Racism (CAWR). Several features of the Toronto-based CAWR are ones I have experienced before. Like many coalitions of our time, CAWR was afflicted by a far-left sectarianism that stifled creativity, risk-taking within the group and its sustainability. This then affected the concurrent problem that is also not uncommon yet receives little to no attention among white activists: how we deal politically and tactically with racism and privilege, both within the group and our political actions. From experience, I would hazard a guess that it was both the sectarianism and the lack of attention to racism that made the coalition unappealing for a number of women of colour who were not seen again after the first few meetings.

As a coalition, we did ensure that demonstration and panel speakers were mainly non-white and we did give attention to having white activists take the lead in dealing with police on street marches, although these decisions were not necessarily made because of overt attention to racism. Perhaps it is not necessary to always discuss anti-racism; maybe it is enough at this point to do it. Yet, although it was never (to my knowledge) discussed in the group or among any white activists, there were also problems with white anti-racism, in terms of process and content, how we functioned in meetings and what we proposed or failed to propose as activities or events.

Also, we did not integrate internal political updates or development into the meetings. This did not help to deal with an unevenness among group members in terms of knowledge, confidence and analysis of what anti-racism meant in this context. For example, the Vancouver publica-tion that started in fall 2001 to cover the war and migrant rights issues from an anti-racist perspective, *Alarm!*, was brought to meetings and read by some individuals, but it could have been applied as an internal educational tool that might have inspired a better organizing strategy. Partly because of this, the coalition was left with a limited get-the-job-done dynamic that could not sustain it: we were there for action and action only. Again, while this was an issue for the coalition as a whole, white activists had the responsibility to improve our own anti-racist practice, which we did not take up.

At more than just one meeting, many of us, as white activists, were too silent at times and at other times talked when we probably should have been listening. That is not to say that people of colour do not do this; it is to say that there is often a common reason why white leftists do, as well as a common form it takes. For example, many of us sit qui-etly, taking in whole meetings. Even when we disagree with a non-white person who is speaking, often anti-racist-conscious white folks do not want to openly do so and so we often do not take part in important political processes, take political risks or take on certain kinds of tasks. We are often content, however, to talk among ourselves after a meeting about how a non-white activist is politically "problematic." On the other hand, the odd white activist in CAWR would give classic long interven-tions on an idea or action, taking up too much highly individualized space and contributing poorly to consensus building. Again, this is not to say that non-white people don't grandstand too. But in my experi-ence as a political white person, I have seen this much more frequently and pervasively among white activists, especially men, as part of that "subjective sensation of superiority."[35] Finally, we had no sense of how to even acknowledge our whiteness and so start to deal with what our roles in the coalition might be, and how they might change at different moments.

The Friends of Grassy Narrows group in Winnipeg seems to be aware of this challenge too. In contrasting their practice with their political principles, Dave Brophy reported that they have yet to determine how to be effective as allies, often being "in a responsive mode" when engaging with Aboriginal activists: "we most often try our best to 'follow the lead.' But this can sometimes be excessive, even paternalistic."[36] Again, this speaks to the necessity for white activists to find new ways to take the political responsibility of engaging with people of colour.

This "ally" concept, which is found in practice in a number of political groups and many community organization-based anti-racist educational activities, is important for white anti-racism. When we apply the concept well, we are taking responsibility and direction at the same time. When we as white activists first acknowledge, then always ask ourselves probing questions about, our position in a multiracial project, we have a good foundation for being an effective ally. For example, when beginning a campaign to fight attacks on migrants, we can ask ourselves things such as, is there funding I can help get or does the fact that I have more free time (due to my independence at work, benefits and pay rate) mean I can fit phone calls, translation or other less exciting administrative work into my schedule better? Could I maybe pitch a fundraising event or panel discussion in networks of mainly white folks who would not otherwise "relate" to the group, and so do my own work of bridging between communities?

Yet, the responsibility-direction balance can tip too far at times with an over-emphasis on seeing ourselves as merely allies and not as interested parties in the struggle. If we really believe that none are truly free until all are free, we must see solidarity relationships as two-way streets and not as forums to which we humbly bring our skills, and in which we will always defer to the opinion of people of colour. Some of the material of the group Colours of Resistance leans in that direction, saying that whites need to keep their mouths shut except when asking questions and see the insights of people of colour as "a very special gift."[37] This is the kind of patronizing trap we can fall in if we do not deal well enough with guilt and fear. Being a good ally does not mean just doing what we're told; it means respecting people of colour and ourselves enough to disagree sometimes and, in doing so, risk finding out that one of us is not right. It means developing together a "better articulation of 'common ground.'"[38]

CAWR also failed to adequately grapple with the key organizing issue of "outreach." The notion of outreach itself and how this is applied was not addressed. Outreach often takes the form of "us" trying to get "others" into a group with a mandate and a program already defined and formed. This is the "we will build it and you will come" kind of outreach. While there is a much more agency-based approach to outreach that sees the legitimacy in starting an activist project, and the need to have that defined and built on how people targeted by racism and war are resisting where they live and work, that approach was not clearly or consistently put forward in this group.

I was part of the outreach committee that was struck a few weeks into the life of the coalition. It was certainly not just poor anti-racism that made this committee flounder, although that is a core part of our inability to make and develop broad community connections. Resolving the movement-building impasses we all face is not the sole responsibility of white activists. But the fact that we do not understand that passing out leaflets on a downtown street corner the week before a demo does not constitute building connections with non-white communities, yet we still actively promote these activities, is telling. Further, when we do sit down in our outreach committees and draw up a list of organizations or community groups that we want to make contact or develop a relationship with, we white activists are often stumped as to who to put on such a list, uncomfortable about figuring out how to make the connections with groups that are suggested and about who should do it, and then, more often than not, silent about acknowledging any of this.

One example of how this played out was our lack of discussion of what it means to contact Muslim groups or organizations. First of all, with essentially no attention given to how we understood religious fundamentalism and what that meant for our work, we were not in a good position for understanding whether there were limits or barriers to whom we wanted to connect with in our outreach. Since Muslims were the primary target of the racism we wanted to combat, the silence on the topic was a big problem. I think this deepened the silence of white anti-racism as well. For example, when suggestions were made in the committee about contacting such-and-such a mosque, or when I saw a Muslim-organized event in an activist newsletter, unconsciously my fear of "looking racist" kicked in and so I did not ask the kinds of questions I would of Christian, Jewish or other faith groups that might have been proposed: "So, who are these different groups? Who do they represent? What are their political positions on the issues?"

What happens to majority white groups in this collective silence is the kind of culture-based polarization I talked about earlier: either a dismissal of all unknown groups and organizations (for example, for not being "radical" enough), or an opportunistic and/or uncritical embracing of all that is Arab and/or Muslim. When this happens in a multiracial setting it is the non-white people who are implicitly left the task of sorting this all out and then doing the bridgework to "their community."[39]

In terms of whiteness and white activist groups that have an anti-fascist focus (such as Anti-Racist Action [ARA] described later), their position or critique of being a majority white group is often not clear. As well, the primary focus on fascism—"Never let the nazis have the streets!"[40]—seems to be lifted from a US context where white supremacy, often especially in the South, has an overt, neo-Nazi character. In Canada, however, while there are neo-Nazi groups to be sure and they must be fought, the form white supremacy and racism takes here at this time is not predominantly that Ku Klux Klan kind.

This is not unlike the *Race Traitor* editors' politics, which wants to transport either mid-nineteenth- or twentieth-century, southern US, abolitionism to the current time and place. Because, while in the 1960s civil rights movement, "whites who directly associated with Blacks inevitably put themselves at risk of being seen as traitors to their race,"[41] forty years later it's not quite the same: every white face is not the enemy and out to kill you.

Also, although white youth are learning and doing something important by putting themselves on the line to fight racism, it seems that direct action tactics are applied as an overall strategy by ARA. These tactics have been employed well in militant case work to, for example, stop deportations, but they do not help us relate to people who are not able (perhaps because of the consequences of racism) or ready to risk arrest. Moreover, if we do not have the broader political conditions — like the solid self-organization of non-status people in Montréal — then direct action may be ineffective or even counter-productive. If it is the only tactic available to us, it is difficult to make ongoing strategic analysis a core part of our struggle, the kind of analysis and political discussion that allows us to decide what is best to do at what time. Such political and strategic analysis needs to be the basis for movement building.

In terms of organized labour, the top-heavy, highly bureaucractic union structure has much to do with how anti-racism is taught and acted on. Many non-white workers are unionized, but their numbers are still low and, not surprisingly, they are generally concentrated in the lowest paid sectors of the workforce. Along with that, there is generally a low consciousness among white workers about white racism itself, and therefore, about our responsibility for figuring out how to do anti-racist education in our locals, how to get the union to adopt effective anti-racist bylaws and policies, how to deal with racist harassment, and how to help more workers of colour become organized.

Combined with that is the myth versus the reality about how labour functions. The myth is that "we are all in it together" as unionists against the power of the boss and that we rank-and-file workers democratically choose and support our local executive boards, our regional and national representatives, and the mother ship of labour, the Canadian Labour Congress, to represent our political and social interests well. While some unions are better than others, the unfortunate reality today is that labour is very top-heavy, with the workers having little real power to influence policy and make critical change. I am militantly pro-union and I have been a steward who was a constant thorn in the side of her employer, as I should have been. But unions as a whole let workers down on many fronts.

What this means in practice is that unionists of colour must doggedly struggle to attain some position of influence or power in order to even begin to be heard about racism. Very few workers of colour are allowed to achieve that position. And once they do, they must rely on each other and the few white allies who fight for anti-racist change. Democratic functioning in unions is often limited to a narrow electoral version and there is often a cycle of fighting to get the candidate in who supports grassroots anti-racism, being able to achieve some successes for a few years when this person is elected, then fighting to keep them in position when officialdom has had enough social change, and, finally, all too often losing ground when the progressive candidate loses and all the policies and programs people fought for are threatened.

As well, very few anti-racist educational efforts get anywhere near the shop floor. If there is a good anti-racist staff person in an influential position who also has an organizing approach, they will make sure workshops are conducted, and that these events are publicized among rank-and-file activists on the shop floor. Yet, often even the most basic education programs happen at conferences that only a few stewards can attend. Often, the same white union activists attend these conferences time and again. Even some of the best organized educational conferences do not integrate anti-oppression training into all their activities, instead organizing workshops on oppression related topics. Participants are allowed to decide not to attend workshops that will challenge them, thus further marginalizing Aboriginal women and women of colour in the process.[42]

Sometimes, officials resist putting effective anti-racism policies in place, to both unionize and then democratically work with workers of colour, and to make white workers and officials accountable for their everyday racism and for their inaction in challenging structural racism. There is much work to be done here.

Finally, whether we are talking about community or workplace organizing, on the left there can be two extremes in terms of building or seeking to build political relationships. In one extreme, much of the far left has a tendency to identify, then dismiss, most community groups or events as mainstream or merely "reformist." This happens in an overly generalized way when *tactics* get mixed up with an overall set of *political goals* and *strategies* for achieving them. That is, if your group is not committed first and foremost to direct action (e.g., building occupations and street takeovers) as your tactic, it is unimportant whether your political goals are to support low-waged workers' organizing or to get some new environmental legislation passed. It matters not to such far leftists that the former would involve an emphasis on grassroots multiracial organizing versus the latter's lobbying in government offices. When tactics and political strategy are conflated like this, and groups are not first committed to direct action as their primary technique, they are not seen as serious about transforming society.

The other extreme happens across the political spectrum of the left. We see white activists lining up behind the person of colour closest to them without making any distinction among political perspectives within different communities of colour or even bothering to find out what a specific group's beliefs or goals are. This is often done, due to an unconscious multiculturalist politic, for access to better numbers at demonstrations, better optics when the media's cameras descend, a basic sense of legitimacy, and/or just to make us feel better about what we're doing.

The goal for better anti-racism, then, is to assess sources of potential political relationships not on either a narrow tactical or a simple identity basis. We owe it to anti-racist struggle to not just exchange one form of objectification for another; we have to uproot the objectification as a whole. To do this, outreach strategies should be political relationship-building ones in which we ask what is our potential for common ground. Everything does not have to be common; we just need some strong potential with which to begin. It does not have to mean developing a complex anti-capitalist platform before we do anything together; we can agree we want to stop racist attacks, poverty wages or exclusion from jobs, and then carry our politics of transformation into the work we do with people.

Such an approach does not mean we give uncritical support to anything any person of colour initiates. Part of the legacy of the culture- and identity-based anti-racism is the implication that whenever people in an oppressed group get together for any reason, that group is seen as inherently progressive. A lot of anti-racist learning and opportunity can be found in social and cultural events, but people of colour, just like white folks, can come together around projects or activities that have little to do with social and political change. As an example, there are a wide range of social service agencies, many of them so committed to their funding sources that they will not do any public political work that will rattle the higher-ups' cages. There are others that manage to fight for their funding and provide good services with an anti-oppression approach by politicized front-line staff who want to do organizing outside work. In coalitions, the former will make themselves known immediately by wanting to talk more about how a campaign fits in with their programs or focussing the entire political strategy on lobbying-type activities. The latter will want to get community people involved right away, as participants and leaders, and suggest ways to make this happen. It's easy to see which dynamic has the potential for a political relationship and which does not.

Where We Learn About Anti-Racism

There are many different forums for anti-racist education and action. Following are some of the kinds of locations where white unionists and activists in Canada generally find ourselves doing our unpaid or paid organizing work and with whom: unions, community agencies, predominantly white and — less frequently — multiracial activist groups that work on projects that are explicitly or implicitly anti-racist, and university or college courses. This selection is meant to be representative, not comprehensive, but it does give the broad range of anti-racist politics to which most white leftists are exposed.

Popular culture, the mass media and the education system all have a huge impact on our anti-racist learning.[43] However, these areas would be whole topics themselves. Therefore, I look specifically at some of the anti-racist learning available to activists and unionists, in activist groups, non-profit community organizations, university courses and within unions. Not surprisingly, there is some theoretical overlap among the sources of learning. For example, many activists are university students so what gets explored in the academy is either explicitly or implicitly carried into activist settings. The same kind of overlap is found with, for example, feminist community organizations and academia, even though the ideas are often presented and developed in a more accessible and/or practical form in community settings than they are taught at university.

Anti-Racist Activism

I highlight the following groups because they have a significant political perspective and impact for anti-racist learning and/or because they
have been active since late 2001. This is important because of how the
intensified attacks on migrants that started then caused an upsurge in
anti-racist activism.

Migrant Rights and Anti-War Organizing

A pan-Canadian group that is a few years old is called No One is Illegal
(NOII). NOII is active, to one degree or another, in several major Canadian cities, namely Montréal, Vancouver, Winnipeg and Toronto.[44] There
is a variety of nation-wide campaigns, from regularization (status for all)
to challenging security certificates to fighting the Safe Third Country
Policy. Along with other migrant rights groups in various Canadian cities,
NOII has taken leadership in making active links between Aboriginal
rights, immigrant and refugee rights and global justice struggles, draw-
ing out "the shared experience of displacement and forced migrations"
to show where "Indigenous peoples' and (im)migrants' lives meet."[45]

The NOII-Montréal group has taken the role of "shepherding self-organization,"[46] as they maintain the communication among, and organization of, a network of twelve different migrant rights groups working
together in early 2005 as "Solidarity Without Borders."[47] The activities
are carried out in a variety of languages. They explicitly seek to carry
out militant, direct action to stop deportations and defend the rights
of non-status people in Canada,[48] through work on individual deportation cases as well as broad-based organizing to challenge anti-migrant
legislation. The group is multiracial, with two-thirds of the collective
being people of colour, and there is a balance of people with and without
status. While the core group is entirely people of colour at this point,
there are several white folks in the broader group, mainly university
students. Sarita Ahooja, the NOII-Montréal member I spoke to, grew up
in a supportive environment to develop an understanding of the value of

militant, community-based organizing. Both her parents were far leftists and active community organizers in the '60s and '70s. Her father was involved in setting up the Asian Friendship Centre at the time of the 1969 race riots in Montréal, while her mom was a nurse and so active with the California grape boycott that Ahooja spent a summer alongside farm workers in the fields when she was two years old.

Ahooja reports that the white people in NOII apply their anti-racist politics in such a way as to be respectful, consultative and seeking of direction. They also "offer their privilege and skills to enhance non-status people's self-organization,"[49] balancing direction and responsibility.

To build the group, they initially carried out monthly assemblies in Montréal neighbourhoods where many migrants lived. NOII-Montréal learned early on, however, that building trusting political relationships with people required starting with more one-on-one connections and word-of-mouth outreach, the kinds of connections that could not be made in an impersonal public meeting.

The Winnipeg NOII group began in late 2003 in response to the threatened deportation of a Syrian man. Although public forums and a conference in the summer of 2004 were attempts at broadening political discussion, group composition and group activities, as of early 2005 this group had essentially become a listserv.[50] This is a common phenomenon of activist groups in our times: a promising start-up with an early denouement. In the NOII-Vancouver composition, there are about twelve people, two-thirds people of colour. And, while there is no rule or explicit mechanism for maintaining this composition, it is "understood that it will remain predominantly people of colour and also take leadership from those who are from immigrant/indigenous communities."[51]

The Coalition Against War and Racism (CAWR) started in the fall of 2001.[52] An ad hoc group of activists had organized a meeting in Toronto City Hall chambers. Politically dissatisfied with the goings on in City Hall,[53] CAWR was the result of a spontaneous side meeting of a multiracial group (a mix of non-white and white people) led by people, particularly women, of colour. The combination of the multiracial and gendered character of the initial group, the passion and the mix of experienced and less-experienced organizers, was a brilliant beginning for an anti-racist project. Our main focus became to carry out actions regarding the then impending war on Afghanistan as well as in response to the general escalation of racism as a result of a specific increase in anti-Arab and -Muslim racism. Our often arduous meetings consisted of planning demonstrations, reaching agreement on slogans and discussing the content of our mandate. The active involvement of many non-white people of various backgrounds was clearly responsible for bringing out a broad-based anti-imperialist analysis as well as maintaining a palpable anger at the racist domestic attacks and international war. As a white anti-racist activist, this was important to me because I wanted to be involved in a multiracial response to the attacks that would promote and sustain the leadership of people of colour, and at the same time, I wanted to share this leadership and responsibility for the work.

Our evolving statement of unity sought to integrate anti-war and -racism struggles with the fight for global justice. The coalition clearly stated Canada's imperialist role in the increasing military adventurism of the US and other allies. And, while we failed to do it, CAWR intended to link this analysis to action by building the movement in neighbourhoods around our city where non-white people targeted by this international and domestic aggression live and work.

Most active around the same time as CAWR, the Heads Up Collective in Toronto was a unique opportunity[54] for anti-racist learning for many white activists. Starting as a sister group to Colours of Resistance (COR) based in Montréal, the leadership of Heads Up was almost entirely young women of colour, and was active in raising awareness work with and for non-status people. They put out a monthly newsletter called *Community Action Notes* and did support work with migrants taken into detention. They explicitly approached their anti-racist work with both an anti-oppression and anti-capitalist framework, seeking to integrate the two for better community activism.

The Heads Up workshop at a New Socialist Group conference I attended in late 2001 was also attended by a number of white youth, several of whom seemed rather nervous about what to say and do but who stayed and worked at it nonetheless. Many more seasoned white activists either chose not to attend the workshop or left just before the small group work that would have required their active participation. Much of the content of the Heads Up anti-oppression analysis is similar to that of non-profit organizations.

The fact that women of colour, like those who lead the Heads Up Collective, do anti-racist education with activists in activist settings can be important for improving our anti-racist organizing. If anti-racist education were ongoing in our groups, and white activists were willing to take on the responsibility of dealing with issues as a core part of our organizing, with young, non-white, women having real leadership in this process, this could lead to change in some of the process and content questions I raised in the section on Organizing for Change. Yet, in that one workshop, it did not seem clear, as in many activist settings, what Heads Up specifically meant by being "anti-capitalist," or how this would connect with an identity-based understanding of oppression.

I found out about their *Community Action Notes* in my work with CAWR. The newsletter states that it is designed to be used as a tool for information-sharing, networking and outreach. As such, it presents a range of happenings, from demonstrations to community agency-based youth events. These happenings represent a breadth of political perspectives that reflects the range, also found among the left as a whole, of opinion about what is to be done and how to do it. The later publications also included reports and analysis on new federal (anti-) immigrant and refugee and anti-terrorist legislation, as well as the history of particular struggles and opinion pieces by people of colour on anti-racism work.

Multiracial Organizing of Low-Wage Workers

Toronto Organizing for Fair Employment (TOFFE) was officially launched toward the end of 2000 as a result of a participatory action research project. Workers involved in that research overwhelmingly said they needed an organization to help them speak out against the erosion of working conditions. TOFFE focussed its energies on two main groups who had shown an interest in organizing: temporary agency workers in a range of low-wage sectors, and contract workers working in community agencies. The evolution of TOFFE (along with the Workers Information Centre) into the Workers' Action Centre (WAC) in May 2005 represents a mounting effort to confront precarious employment, broadly defined, with worker-centred organization.[55]

WAC now has seven staff from Tamil, Chinese, Spanish-speaking, and South Asian communities, as well as 2000 people in their database, with forty to fifty active members on various working committees, and sixty to seventy members who attend their regular members' meetings. The Board of Directors, while a majority of white people when the organization started as TOFFE, has evolved in its racial composition and community representation as the organization develops and more workers become members and directors. Emily Chan, a TOFFE staff person, states that part of the reason for this evolution has been the organizational shift to focus more on action and less on research as the top priority. The membership is a majority of immigrants of colour because "since we're focussing on low wages, that's who comes in"[56] to the centre. This focus on workers and/or immigrants of colour has been the organization's mandate from day one.

While TOFFE used to hold monthly drop-in meetings in different neighbourhoods, for which they did general leafleting in each area, they had a similar experience to that of NOII-Montréal. It was difficult to connect and develop relationships with people in that kind of setting, with that kind of method. So they started to focus even more on community/language-specific media to get the word out about TOFFE's services to affected workers. In 2002, a group of door-to-door sales workers subcontracted by Rogers Cable sought TOFFE's support for getting unpaid back wages. A two-year fight ensued that used a multi-pronged strategy of filing official complaints with the Ministry of Labour, raising public awareness through leafleting at Rogers's stores, creative demonstrations outside of the Rogers head office and targeted phone campaigns. The hard work and determination paid off: in 2004 all the workers were paid the money they were owed by the third party that had subcontracted them.[57] WAC's approach has become one of developing such campaigns based on the many workers who now call or drop in to their centre. Given that there is still $19 million in unpaid wages that the Ontario Ministry of Labour has failed to collect over the last two years, WAC's work will only become more important.

Aboriginal Solidarity Work

White folks have at times done anti-racist activism in solidarity with Aboriginal people. One of the biggest and most significant Aboriginal uprisings of our time was that of the Mohawks of Kanehsatake in 1990. A current example of Aboriginal organizing is the Grassy Narrows First Nation blockade and the solidarity of Friends of Grassy Narrows group in Winnipeg with it.[58]

The solidarity activities of the Friends are to raise public awareness about the Grassy Narrows' struggle for self-determination and their land through local events and forums, provide support at the Grassy Narrows First Nation's blockade, write articles and organize demonstrations. There are three white men in the core group and, while at the first meeting, twenty-five people came out, in early 2005 there are about a dozen other people involved in some way. These include a few Aboriginal and South Asian people, and a majority of white group members. One of the three core group members, Dave Brophy reports that he became drawn to Aboriginal solidarity work while working for an organization in Peru that focussed on indigenous rights. The group has developed "working relationships with several Native-led political organizations," but they have found it challenging to build the group.[59] Brophy further comments that, while the political relationships formed within the Friends are few and not overly well developed, the efforts at interracial solidarity in Winnipeg are important nonetheless. In fact, they have co-organized various events with Native political organizations in that city, resulting in good political relationships that could lead somewhere in the future. The Friends do not have an explicit anti-racist politic, but are committed "to expose, condemn and resist the systemic racism faced by indigenous peoples in Canada," especially with respect to rights "of control over, and even access to, their own land."[60] Brophy admits that this message has yet to get out beyond the far left.

Anti-Racism in General Organizing

As mentioned above, Colours of Resistance (COR) is a "grassroots network of people who actively work to develop multiracial, anti-racist politics in the movement against global capitalism."[61] Their efforts are focussed mainly in a Web site dedicated to providing analysis and organizing tools. There you can find serious efforts at improving white anti-racism, not only by helping to understand the problem but by giving practical tools on how to be an effective ally to people of colour. Learning how to deal with defensiveness and guilt, how/when to challenge racist behaviour and how to sort out when to lead and when to follow are all important potential areas of an ally component of such trainings. Definitions, analyses and tools on the site are written by both white and non-white people.

Anti-Racist Action (ARA) has 150 chapters in the US and Canada. In Toronto, at least, it has attracted many white youth who are looking for a place to fight fascism and racism with people they can relate to culturally. The members are "people from all different backgrounds with all different viewpoints," but there are a set of principles on which the group is based: ARA will fight fascists wherever they are active; they rely on each other for protection, not the cops; ARA will defend and support the actions of other anti-fascist groups; and they are pro-choice and work within in a broad anti-oppression framework.[62]

Tactically, ARA has been a direct-action-oriented group. They state that they put themselves physically on the line to protest fascism and racism, even if police brutality is the result. By 2005 the group seems to exist more as a social network than a political group, but a few years ago, the Toronto chapter was actively involved in supporting the Ontario Coalition Against Poverty (OCAP). As a result, anyone joining the group was bound to learn that seriously fighting racism requires personal risk, something even working-class whites may not understand. Given that police will generally treat white folks less harshly than people of colour, white youth learn first hand about how to use their privilege to fight oppression.

The International Socialists (IS) is not a specifically anti-racist group, but their perspective on racism is important to look at because of the significant number of white activists who work in and with that organization and because the IS does have a clear set of anti-racist politics. Not surprisingly, the IS understanding of racism is firmly rooted in a structural analysis of the functioning of capitalism, in which racism is said to be a feature of capitalism that brings about "systemic inequalities in power and life chances."[63] From this perspective, Marxists "regard racism as a product of capitalism which serves to reproduce the social system by dividing the working class; it can be abolished, but only through a socialist revolution achieved by a united working class, one in which blacks and whites join together against their common exploiter." Racism is also seen as arising from the myth that biological differences exist among humans, making some naturally inferior to others. This was later largely replaced with cultural racism. Therefore, the IS position is that racism is a "historical novelty" of capitalist societies. That is, it does not pre-date capitalism and has no pre-capitalist historical roots in the various forms of "prejudices amongst strangers" or inter-religious prejudices. It is about "capitalism's reliance on slave labour (becoming) an anomaly requiring explanation."[64]

In terms of the white privilege that many anti-racists understand to be part of racism, this view holds that white workers do not derive any material benefit from racism. Rather, the ruling class has created hate and fear among non-white and white workers, driving a wedge between us: we have no inherent interest in oppressing Blacks. Instead, we get a "'public and psychological wage' for being 'part of white nation building.'"[65] As well, the white working class can use racism to explain economic crises and be able to blame them on someone who is not the ruling class. These ideas fit with the Agency and Structure theme I analyzed in the first section of this chapter.

This understanding of racism is not unique to the IS. Many people on the far left hold this or a slightly less narrow version of this view. It is common not only to white socialists but to non-white far leftists coming from particular political currents.

Non-Profit Community Organizations

Much anti-oppression work in the last few decades in community organizations results from the political demands of women of colour. In Toronto, a pivotal event that had a ripple effect to other geographical locations and for years to come was the 1986 International Women's Day organizing. The women of colour involved in the organizing, such as the Black Women's Collective, demanded a more systemic anti-racist practice through outreach, diversification and representation in structures.[66] White women resisted change then, and many still do today, as many of us continue to benefit from privileged positions in the social hierarchy. In fact, "attempts to alter shelter, crisis lines, immigrant women's services and cultural institutions were met with resistance and hostility, struggles that often were well covered by Canadian newspapers."[67]

Despite the opposition, serious anti-oppression work has continued in many community organizations, where multiracial, multi sexual orientation, and mixed-class leadership and memberships have been developed. White women involved as volunteers or staff of these organizations are often required to follow explicit anti-racism policies and are expected to take the anti-racism and -oppression trainings offered by such organizations. Because most of this work is being done in feminist organizations, it is fair to say that very few white men receive the challenge and benefit from such training. Many other community organizations have yet to take anti-racism work seriously, and take on instead "diversity training."

The content of the anti-racist training generally offers white people an opportunity to understand various forms of oppression and privilege and locate ourselves within these. Capitalism, slavery and colonialism are usually put forward as systems of domination that are related to or bring about these forms of oppression. Fundamental to this work is personalizing privilege and oppression for taking responsibility for our individual oppressive behaviour as whites, but also to "stress that women are the experts of their experience and if given the tools of analysis and problem solving can arrive at positive solutions for themselves and others."[68] This is essential to agency and so very important. As well, the concepts of cultural and other types of identities and difference are used to grapple with our multiple and different locations in society. For example, I am oppressed as a woman, but privileged by white skin/Anglo-Saxon origins and a heterosexual orientation. We then can look at how the various identities of race, class and gender have an impact on us. While this is a positive thing, these trainings often fail to integrate this identity-analysis in a social relations framework that understands the complexity of the issue of difference.

The community organization trainings are often multiracial and there are exercises that participants must do separately and together. In the most basic way, these put whites in the position of confronting our racist stereotypes and the invisibility of our white privilege. We have to work with women of colour on this and deal with it somehow. Often, anti-racism trainings in non-profit organizations also include discussion on how to be an ally. This is also an important concept and approach to anti-racist work, when understood in a full way: there is much more to being an ally than just figuring out what is the "right" thing to do.

Academic Approaches

In universities, as well as some college programs, there are many different works and teachings on anti-racism. I have chosen to focus on the ones below specifically as a result of following a trail of political breadcrumbs back from what I have heard and seen in activist group meetings, events and demonstrations over the years. There are particular schools of thought that have had a major impact on our understanding of racism and application of an anti-racist politic. It seems to me that we can define three broad academic sources today: anti-racist feminism, postmodernism and whiteness studies. Clearly, there is overlap between these but they have specific features as categories worth looking at as significant influences, both on white activists who spend time in post-secondary study and on community-based anti-racist education.

Anti-Racist Feminism

Anti-racist feminism, which has been the foundation of my own political development, can be said to "(stem) from women of colour's willingness to strive for equality in a racialized society and feminist movement."[69] Within the large body of work on anti-racist feminism is a wide range of perspectives that range from a strict epistemology approach to a purely political economy approach. That is, they range from those perspectives that see knowledge of oppression and what to do about it as fundamentally (and sometimes only) starting from oppressed peoples' lives — their experience and agency — to those theories that see repressive and exploitive international and domestic structures as being the starting point for analysis and action.

My own take fits somewhere in the middle of that spectrum in the form of an anti-racist feminist socialism. However, when I was first developing my anti-racism, I would say I was more on the epistemology or "identity-is-all" end of the spectrum. This ties in with what I have been describing at different points in this book about why people — and not just whites — are without a multilayered framework of analysis. If we are too focussed on a limited understanding of identity, we are missing the historically connected material conditions that set the stage within which we are acting. Although that acting has an impact on what the stage continues to look like, the degree and nature of the impact will vary with time and place. The "identity-is-all" approach left us with no way to see our circumstances fully and, therefore, to see our full humanity.

In terms of the academic influences on my shift on the anti-racist feminist continuum, a few Canadian feminist scholars have influenced me. I particularly remember reading Himani Bannerji as my first experience with a feminism that really integrated both racism and a class analysis in a fundamental way. The only way I can describe that experience was suddenly feeling theoretically more at home. At the time, I was trying to develop an analysis of capitalism and class but I had always felt alienated from the reductionist approaches of the most visible socialists. The most extreme of them think there is no integration between the various systems of oppression and exploitation: for them the issue is class and class only, and they seem to believe that freedom from capitalism will automatically bring an end to oppression.

Postmodernism

The postmodernist philosophy not only permeates most areas of university study today but has filtered into popular culture and the language and functioning of business. At the same time, "No one exactly agrees as to what is meant by the term, except, perhaps that 'postmodernism' represents some kind of reaction to, or departure from, 'modernism'. Since the meaning of modernism is also very confused, the reaction or departure known as 'postmodernism' is doubly so."[70] Even so, there is a set of concepts that generally reflects what a large part of the left has come to understand about postmodernism. Although this understanding may be overly boiled down, in my experience it is this set of ideas that influence and/or are reflected in some of the more identity- and difference-based community anti-racism or diversity training. We generally have postmodernism to thank for pulling the rug out from under an integrated social relations perspective on how human beings relate to each other. If modernism is seen as overly rational, absolute, technocratic and focussed on progress, postmodernism is meant to liberate us from our dissatisfaction with "nature and the limits of Western modernity"[71] through embracing heterogeneity and difference.

Kenan Malik states that postmodernism evolved in the 1980s "as the intellectual embodiment of (the) social fragmentation" that was being experienced in many Western societies,[72] the roots of which were set down well before. The early optimism offered by objective science and universal morality coming out of the secular Enlightenment was sorely damaged in the first half of twentieth century by Hitler's Germany, Stalin's Russia, and the US nuclear attack on Hiroshima and Nagasaki, and was further frustrated by the disappointing decline of social movements in the mid-1970s. This all opened the door to postmodern theorizing, which suggests that to move beyond this horror and defeat we had to leave behind notions of universalism and accept fragmentation. Some of the key features of the fragmentation approach are:

- *No Universality*: There is no universal analysis for understanding the world — often termed grand or meta narratives — so we cannot see or understand society as a totalizing whole. As a result, social reality cannot be directed or determined by one big factor such as the economy. Another apparent problem with the universal is that it is associated with Western origins of modernity and so is inherently Eurocentric and repressive.

- *Deconstruction*: Western modernity created internal and external "others" and continues to form and reconstruct these to keep some people marginalized and others privileged. The postmodern thinker Derrida proposes "deconstruction" — a pulling apart of how things are talked about and believed — to show how false binary poles "in Western discourses and cultural identities such as male/female, active/passive, culture/nature, civilized/savage, white/black" are set up.[73]

- *Difference and identity*: There is a focus on difference among social groups so that the particular history and identity of each group firmly sets them apart from others. Difference is given such importance that there becomes no need to grapple with the fragmentation that first exists and then is deepened by this privileging. As people (subjects) are decentred and de-essentialized through this process, many potential free flowing identities are available to the subject. Our understanding of things that happen in society is therefore also decentred. For example, definitions of ethnicity and racism are terms that "are permanently in between, caught in the impossibility of fixity and essentialization."[74] Culture is included as one of these identities that are in flux and so is apparently not tradition-bound.

- *Power and discourse*: As with knowledge and understanding, power is not fixed but moves through shifting realities; for example, the construction of racialized identities through various discourses — how things are talked about or represented — or the internally divided and fragmented power of state and capital.

Clearly some of these ideas are problematic. While social systems do evolve and change over time, this does not mean the power relations that run through them become released from their moorings. If we see power as being so unfixed and identities are so freely chosen, then how are we to understand the tenacious, complex and contradictory functioning of systems of domination?

Whiteness Studies

Whiteness, as an area of anti-racism theory, varies widely. Naming and analyzing whiteness is an important step for white anti-racism, and doing so without further privileging it and entrenching the idea of a "white race." We must focus on whiteness to see how those of us who have been socially constructed as being white are "racialized for preferential treatment."[75] One area of whiteness study does this through tracing this history of social construction in the context of the development of capitalism, with the focus on how white supremacy and privilege are handed out to, and accepted by, the working class. Given the integration of white supremacy with capitalism in much of whiteness theory, it seems that more and more of the far left today is looking at these kinds of analyses for their anti-racist learning.

Many academics who draw on whiteness theory understand the development and maintenance of white working-class racism as arising from the need to explain our exploitation. We can blame the non-white worker nearest us for our poor situation, rather than looking at the rich as the problem. Vic Satzewich gives the example of the virulent white racism in northern Ontario towards Aboriginal peoples as the northern white worker is frustrated by the southern Ontario white worker's better circumstances.[76] Many whiteness theorists say that the Irish who emigrated to the US in the late nineteenth and early twentieth centuries "became white" because, in taking on and accepting whiteness, they received a public and psychological wage and/or some real improvement in their lives. At that time, whiteness "offered a way for the newly formed working class to express fears of dependency and anguish over the imposition of capitalist discipline,"[77] and "racialized imagery and stereotypes ... provide tools with which workers make sense of their daily experience."[78]

At the same time, the ruling class plays a key role in much of whiteness theory. Some whiteness perspectives say that racism came out of slavery in the US. It was Africans who were enslaved, not because they were Black, but because capitalists needed unfree labour—the cheapest kind—for activities like cash cropping. Once that system was in place, theories about racial inferiority were developed to justify slavery. As an extension of that, Italian, Irish and eastern European immigrant workers in the US in the late 1800s to early 1920s were "ascribed (a) racial identity" in the legal system and popular culture, where there was a "formal racial ideology" that placed them below whites but just above African- and Asian-Americans.[79] Their position at that time, in relation to whiteness, can be called "not-yet-white" or "off-white" ethnics. In Canada, eastern and southern European groups also "became white" eventually,[80] also taking on the associated white supremacy and racism.

In early twentieth-century Canada, Ukrainians were deemed to be "racially suited for the difficult work of pioneer farming on the Prairies" while Italians were 'suited' to "the difficult, back-breaking and dirty work of building the urban infrastructures of Canada's major cities."[81] The first working-class white settlers were escaping poverty, social and religious exclusion, and constraint, and most came as free labour whereas most non-white workers came as slaves or bonded labourers, and "were often constrained in North America by legal restrictions placed upon their movements and activities."[82]

As a result of "political and ideological manoeuvers"[83] to satisfy the pro-slavery objectives of the US plantation-connected ruling class in the nineteenth century, Irish Catholics were "sea-changed into 'white Americans'."[84] The ruling-class message to Irish workers was that if slavery ended, African-Americans would be competing with white workers for jobs. There was more than just a message: the number and kinds of privileges for working-class Irish were increased, ranging from shorter prison sentences to actual cash payments if they voted pro-slavery. Irish-

Americans bought this and supported the anti-abolitionist side, thereby taking on white supremacy in "a country that was already structured on racial lines."[85] And so they became "implicitly enrolled in the system of racial oppression of all African-Americans."[86] The outright social apartheid in both Canada and the US that existed until not too many decades ago was often imposed by such overt ruling-class choices as a means of social control.

Even before the American civil war, whites were constitutionally free to emigrate and obtain US citizenship, whereas non-whites were not. In the eighteenth century the poorest European-American was in a better situation than free African-Americans: "The United States Constitution implicitly made immigration a white-skin privilege, when in Article I, Section 9, Europeans were classed as migrants, whilst Africans were classed as imports."[87] Even when the original article was repealed in 1790, it still provided that "any alien, being a free white person" could become a US citizen.

In 1950s and 1960s Canada, immigrant farm workers came as either free immigrants or unfree migrants, thereby getting either permanent or temporary entry privileges. While Black workers gained only the latter, due to their supposed incompatibility with "full participation in Canadian society," white workers from Holland were free and landed as "government officials felt that as members of the 'White race' their 'initiative' and 'love of freedom' could not in good conscience be contained."[88]

One way that whiteness theory applies to radical practice is found in the above-mentioned US-based *Race Traitor* publications. The editors' goal is to "focus on whiteness and the struggle to abolish the white race from within,"[89] although contributions to the journal vary significantly from the editors' view. Once there are enough defectors from the white race, the system will collapse. The term "race traitor" comes from their position that "a traitor to the white race is someone who is nominally classified as white, but who defies the rules of whiteness so flagrantly as to jeopardize his or her ability to draw upon the privileges of white skin."[90] The editors challenge the use of the term "racism" because it arises from a falsely constructed social category, race. The editors also claim that all anti-racists are too liberal, seeking reforms within the law and order agenda. Instead, they see themselves as abolitionists, continuing on in the US tradition of centuries before.[91]

They also have a strong focus on rejecting some and taking on other specific forms of culture as being important for abolitionism. In the US context, they hold that giving up whiteness, "crossing over," can occur getting into basketball, hip-hop and other African-American-identified sporting and cultural activities. This comes as a result of seeing white culture as other anti-racist whites do: empty, violent and a strong basis for white supremacy.[92]

Labour
The word "labour" is commonly used to refer to the organizations of unionized workers. Labour has a functioning and internal political culture that is, in many ways, distinct from community organizations. There is much variation among different unions — often due to their own particular history of racialized development — with respect to how seriously they take anti-racism, in terms of allocating resources, making structural changes in staffing, democratic functioning and organizing priorities.[93]

There are unions that organize in sectors where there are high numbers of low-paid women of colour, and in doing so, integrate some basic anti-racism into their organizing strategy. They translate materials into the workers' first languages, provide some transportation costs, meet with the workers in their homes and may even hire women of colour in small numbers and/or on a contract basis to be involved in the organizing. Yet, in the big picture, such unions still do not generally open doors for involvement and leadership by workers of colour within their union once they are organized, and so both the elected union leadership and the permanent staff representatives to the locals tend to be overwhelmingly white and male.

Some unions do take anti-racist education seriously, often, as we discussed earlier in Organizing for Change, with mixed results. For example, the Canadian Auto Workers Union (CAW) devotes resources to an education department, a site to do the training, and paid time off for both workers and their families to attend single- or multi-week courses.

One tool used by the CAW for anti-racist education is the "Teach Me to Thunder" train-the-trainer manual for building anti-racist, grassroots union leaderships. This manual locates the training in a social relations framework that also looks historically at repression of Aboriginal peoples and non-white migrants. The training's goals include getting participants to: understand and change their biases and attitudes; challenge oppressive and exploitative social relations; not use anti-racist education for the state to manage racism better; ensure that whites don't just get individual "personal growth opportunities" instead of struggling for social change; and, learn to be anti-racist, not pro-multiculturalist.[94] White participants in this training must therefore deal first hand and hands-on with their own biases, racism and privilege. But such training opportunities are not necessarily widely available for shop floor activists.

A union with unique anti-racist activity is the Public Service Alliance of Canada (PSAC).[95] With respect to hiring union staff, they have a true employment equity policy. They will hire outside the union to ensure that Aboriginal and/or workers of colour are employed in designated positions. The increasing number of non-white staff was significant enough to lead to a recent national "Aboriginal and Workers of Colour Staff Conference," an event previously unheard-of in the union movement.

Nonetheless the union structure and poor democratic functioning make these successes fragile. The PSAC "component" (or sub-local) structure separates PSAC workers by job sector, mimicking the organization of government. This compromises solidarity within the union as workers see their interests from component to component as being separate. And, while PSAC is relatively democratic, members and staff are still hamstrung by a top-heavy officialdom, and must fight to get a progressive leader into power for a short period of time and then work hard to make as much change as possible while she's there. As PSAC negotiator Carol Wall put it, "It's no surprise that workers of colour are reluctant to become unionized even when unions seek them out. Who wants to be part of a union you're not really part of?"[96]

The Canadian Union of Public Employees (CUPE) is a good example of how the nature of anti-racism work and the ability to do it are related to the size of a union local, its structure and the composition of its membership.[97] Currently, at the national level of the union, their Web site indicates an understanding of the problems racism creates for workers.[98] From the principles outlined there, it is clear the union officially has a systemic understanding of racism: both about the way workers of colour are treated on a day-to-day basis and also about the way they are structured into low-waged work and so often excluded from unionized positions. The union also seems to understand that a three-pronged solution is required: getting anti-racist language into collective agreements, making the unionization of workers of colour a priority and building strong union-community relationships. The Web site also reports that in May 2005 there was a workers of colour conference to strike a plan to organize "to strengthen CUPE's diversity and membership." They specifically sought to train workshop attendees to be "member-organizers" for future campaigns.

It is not clear, though, with what longevity and how consistently this translates into action and supports rank-and-file organizing at the local level. For example, while education is supposed to be a priority in the union for moving forward on social justice issues, a quick survey of the list of 2005 workshops offered across the country reveals that in only one province is there one workshop addressing racism.[99] Further, Stephanie Ross reports that when she was on CUPE District Council in Toronto, they tried to offer a new equity workshop a number of times but always had to cancel it because of too few registrations.[100] This is even given that the strongly stated anti-racist organizing agenda has been part of the union for some years.

Nonetheless, many locals forge ahead with anti-racist activity from the bottom up. It is interesting to contrast two examples: CUPE 3903 and CUPE 79. The former is a local of more than 2400 members, teaching assistants and contract faculty at York University in Toronto. Both the nature of the membership and the often radical environment of student life at York affect the character of anti-racist activity in that setting. For example, there was an upsurge in union anti-racism work in the post-9/11 wake of the rise of Zionist lobby at York after a September 2002 Concordia University pro-Palestinian protest caused former Israeli Prime Minister Netanyahu's talk to be cancelled.[101]

In contrast, CUPE 79 is a union of more than 20,000 City of Toronto "inside" municipal workers. It has many different units, depending on the sector of work. These include workers in recreation and homes for the aged, public-health workers and cleaners, to mention just a few. For many of these members, anti-racist work is seen at the bargaining table and in militant shop-floor activity or public protests. One example of the strong organizing of workers of colour is that of the cleaners in 2004. As the first unit on the privatization chopping block, they led a non-contracting-out fight-back and won. Their message made clear links: we are marginalized as both immigrants and low-wage workers, and one has to do with the other.[102] The contrast of these two locals shows how workers' conditions — such as their wages, their work sector, their environment, and their vulnerability to the employer — influence greatly the kind of anti-racist struggles in which they will engage.

The local, regional and national labour federations also vary in their approach to anti-racist work. The Ontario Federation of Labour (OFL) has a seminar for stewards and staff that makes taking racial harassment seriously a legal obligation; that is, if people cannot change attitudes, perhaps fear of personal legal liability for failing to act will help.[103] As well, the Canadian Labour Congress (CLC) has carried out a number of anti-racist trainings, research and education projects for and about women workers and, more recently, Aboriginal and worker of colour conferences.[104]

One result of this is the CLC's 1997 report, *Challenging Racism: Going Beyond Recommendations* and the 1998 follow-up CLC First National Aboriginal/Workers of Colour Conference. The documents that resulted from the hard work of mainly non-white workers are meant to be educational and action tools. The 1997 report not only analyzes racism in the union bureaucracy and in society as a whole, with a working class focus as well, but it also puts forward a list of recommendations for addressing this.

Some of the many of recommendations from the 1998 conference include: link homelessness and poverty with racism; integrate an anti-racist perspective in all union work; increase the levels of staffing; carry out public grassroots campaigns; and, make key structural changes in the union, such as adopting anti-racist action plans and improving internal union democracy.[105] While many of these make a strong union-community connection, they seem to lack an organizing framework from which to carry them out. The report's conclusion is that CLC will continue to work on implementing the report and unions, at every level, will do the same. But an organizing framework is one in which there is a clear strategy for achieving grassroots involvement in development and implementation of a social change project. If the conference itself recognized that the union structure and functioning are lacking in democracy, and racism is part of that structure, a brief statement of political will on the part of the CLC is not going to be enough to make change. A commitment to hard timelines, increased staffing and other financial resources would be part of a organizing strategy, as would a clear program for increasing member of colour involvement in the implementation of the recommendations.

Pointing the Way to Better White Anti-Racism

These past chapters have been leading to pointing the way to better anti-racism. To this end, developing the analytical framework laid out in Chapter One has meant covering a lot of different ground. As described in that chapter, the point of the framework is to integrate social processes involving racism and anti-racism in three ways:

- in the relationship between everyday and structural forms of white racism;

- in terms of the various power relations and how we experience them, particularly racism, sexism and class-exploitation; and,

- with respect to how these power relations function and are reproduced within the historical context of imperialism and capitalism.

The interconnection of these three processes has been revealed through tracing the complex evolution from othering to racism in the Canadian-specific context. We have also seen how, today, everyday street-level attacks on people of colour, and workplace 'polite' racism, are deeply interconnected with neo-liberal (re)structuring of precarious work and migrants' access to legal status. The complexity of Canada's place in the functioning of international capitalism not only creates challenges for the ruling class regarding managing racism; it also has a significant impact on our will and ability to understand the methods and dynamics of racism for social control, and then to find the social space to challenge and change it.

This is our ongoing challenge, then: to recognize and analyze the limits and opportunities that particular social conditions present to us in our place and time, then to find and create the social space within these to ease the pressure of racist practices and programs, but, more importantly, to build broad-based movements leading to the transformation of our society to one in which racism would have little chance of continued existence.

To that end, the final chapter will look at a number of examples of current organizing from which we can learn and take inspiration, and on which we can build. To lead us into that, what follows is a summary of some of the important points developed in the previous chapters, presented in the form of principles that can serve to guide us in our work.

Anti-Racist Organizing Principles

Framework Principles

- Make a long-term commitment to fight racism where it happens, both the everyday and the structural.

- Analyze social relations to see how various kinds of power are formed, become systemic, are carried out over time, and how they overlap and interconnect. Carry history into the present.

- Know which side of the class fence we are on, who is there with us, and in what conditions we all are living and working.

- Analyze the political context, and assess the challenges and possibilities for our agency.

- Remember that anti-racism is not about food and dance. Honour and support expressions of identity but know that our work is not based on simple notions of difference, but, rather, about power. This means challenging the multiculturalists' race relations approach to racism.

- Look for ways to challenge our membership in the white supremacy club and to undermine that sensation of superiority.

- Inventory the "invisible knapsack": continually assess and challenge our privilege and assumptions. Deal with the fascination and guilt, the shame and despair we have with our position, and engage in respectful self-criticism. Remember that there's no way around it but through it.

- Share our analyses, what we have learned and ideas for better anti-racist action, not just with each other as whites but in our work with non-white organizers too.

- Be open to use of all kinds of tactics, depending on what will get the job done at that time. This means re-defining "radical." It's not a just a conviction or a lifestyle: it's a willingness to struggle.

- Think of all organizing as anti-racist organizing.

"Who to Work With" Principles

- Seek out and encourage the development of multiracial settings that include Aboriginal people, people of colour and whites.

- Develop political relationships with people of colour based on working towards shared political goals, not superficial short-term alliances or narrow ideas of social or cultural identities.

- Get involved in building an anti-racist movement based on participation and leadership by women of colour.

- Be an effective ally by seeing fighting racism as in our interest as whites too and by constantly sorting out when to lead and when to follow in this fight.

- Seek out other anti-racist whites as our allies, especially in majority-white environments.

Democratic Functioning Principles

- Understand that democracy means having a voice, responsibility and power, from the bottom up. This cannot be handed out from self-appointed movement leaders, regardless of whether they are people of colour. Clear decision-making structures and processes must be set up for this.

- Be accountable to each other.

- Challenge sectarianism.

- Understand that we do not have all the answers.

- Practise listening and talking just a little bit less. At the same time, understand that taking direction does not mean being silent and just letting someone tell us what to do.

- Be as open to useful criticism as we are to compliments.

Making White Anti-Racist Organizing Better: Where To From Here?

Introduction

There is no one organizing formula for building an effective, solid anti-racist movement. Developing a strategy depends on many factors, including the time and place we are in, what kinds of existing political relationships and allies we have, and what broad social conditions exist as a consequence of history.

The range of effectiveness of the No One Is Illegal (NOII) groups across Canada demonstrates why developing an effective strategy is so complex. In contrast to NOII-Winnipeg's start with organizing around the case of one person, NOII-Montréal's success at applying their clear anti-racist political strategy is because of the self-organization of targeted communities. This is a fundamental condition for successful movement building and, in Canada, not one that easily presents itself these days. But it was the state's targeting of the sizeable Algerian migrant population in Quebec that paved the way for the Action Committee of Non-Status Algerians to develop in late 2001. There was a large community, from the same country of origin, most of whom were about to be directly affected by the state's planned deportation of non-status Algerians. A number of them had been politically active in Algeria.

Theirs was a struggle with the most grave consequences for many people living in a specific geographic location. After laying groundwork, what catapulted them to national attention was one family's taking refuge in a church in October 2002. What they won was a partial regularization program. At the end of the day, 83% of the Algerian Quebeckers fit the federal program's criteria.[1] Sarita Ahooja also reported that their community-specific struggle was demobilized after this, leaving the other 17% without the full support that the whole group previously had had.

The very public and militant activities developed a relationship between the Algerians and community activists with status and has led to broadening the movement to include migrants from Colombia, Palestine, Somalia, Egypt and South Asia, who are currently active in the Solidarity Without Borders network. This locally based multiracial movement, along with the work of immigrant workers' centres, such as WAC in Canada as well as others in the US, offers us some hopeful models for broadening anti-racist movement building in terms of the local quality of the work but, at some point, we hope, with respect to a national scope.

With that hopefulness in mind, it's useful to reflect on possibility. We are not in a moment in history that makes fundamental social transformation likely in the near future, although many of us firmly believe that this is what is needed for true social and political change. There is a notable absence of good education about political organizing in Canada, but the problem is much bigger than that. The economic and political forms of capitalism and imperialism give the right a solid hold on global and local power, making day-to-day life and collective action more and more difficult for most people. From Canadian politicians who were against a lone US attack on Iraq but were fine with a pseudo UN-led massacre and later occupation, to the government position that we have an Employment Insurance surplus simply because rates have been too high rather than because eligibility has been sharply restricted, to the multi-layered legislative efforts to persecute most migrants of colour, we see a ruling class committed to marginalizing more and more of the population to maintain and improve the elites' favourable place in the world hierarchy. These attacks have many fronts and are devastating. At the same time, much of the international left (in different conditions and circumstances) ranges from being unable or unwilling to grapple, in a broad and serious way, with where we are at and what we continue to do at present.

Even so, it is still important to look at what we might be able to do differently in Canada, to be encouraged by the organizing successes we do see, and to look for opportunities to try to broaden these successes. At the very least, while we cannot ignore or completely change the overall conditions of our struggle, we can work on having an anti-racist orientation to all the racist material we come across each day, and actively challenge racism, as well as pursue organized, anti-racist, political activities.

Therefore, as white unionists and activists, here are two fronts to work on at the same time:

- *Individual and Collective Challenges to Racism*: Even without a broad-based movement, we can take on the incidents of everyday racism that go on around us, we can challenge our own and each other's white supremacy and racism, and we can act in our communities and workplaces to challenge the structural racism that often comes in the form of policies and programs, or lack thereof.

- *Anti-Racist Organizing for Broad Social Change*: This is a tough challenge, but we can try to organize in communities, workplaces and unions with this broad goal in mind, while recognizing it is a step-by-step process with often externally imposed limits. To be effective, this action needs to be done within an *integrated, anti-racist, organizing framework*, as demonstrated by how we set and work towards our political goals, whom we choose to work with, who the leadership of our projects is, and what projects we choose to work in and/or politically support.

Individual and Collective Challenges to Racism

An active commitment to daily anti-racist acts means that we take on white racism in the workplace, with our neighbours, and with family and friends, when it surfaces in attitudes or is implemented in structures. Here are only a few examples of the range of actions this can mean:

- challenging casual remarks that anti-terrorism measures are legitimate security efforts that protect us all. This can be a hard thing to do because the anti-terrorism discourse has become so prevalent — after the response to September 11, 2001, it became quite quickly "the way things are."

- challenging so-called subtle racist behaviours such as co-workers silently leaving the room every time a Black customer or client enters. This co-worker may never use hard-core racist language, may never say something overt about their racism, but, in the framework of "polite" Canadian racism, patterns of avoidance behaviour do show themselves and can be uncovered.

- providing public support to rank-and-file unionists of colour targeted by acts of racism, and taking their lead in how they want to respond. It may well mean risking being ostracized by other white unionists, maybe friends and workplace allies in other situations, and even our advancement within the union.

- advocating for employment equity and anti-discrimination policies.

- negotiating anti-racist policies in collective agreements.

- getting effective anti-racism workshops at our union locals.

- condemning a racist poster in a store or a submission to a community group newsletter, without waiting to see what people of colour will do or say.

- supporting women of colour who say they need a women's caucus to discuss their experience of exclusion in a shared multiracial political group, even if, as white women, we do not feel this same marginalization.

This last situation exemplifies an opportunity for challenging the integration of racism and sexism. In one group I was involved with, I did not feel that marginalization because of how racism and sexism were integrated in such a way that the sexism was different for women of colour than for the white women.[2] This played out in many ways, including unspoken alliances between white women and men of colour, both to maintain power and control of a project and also because the former fear hearing about their racism and the latter about their sexism. Supporting women of colour in that situation meant being prepared to take on directly what ranged from defensiveness to outright paranoia ("I am being attacked/excluded; why are they having meetings themselves?") of both white women and most men in the group, as well as taking the opportunity to see how we ourselves were participating in that exclusion, whether actively or passively, consciously or not, and then taking steps to do things differently.

All this means a lot of intervention in the day-to-day dialogue that reflects how whites continually put out and reinforce our understanding of "the way things are." It means taking a lot of risks, especially in social, family or workplace settings. Doing these kinds of things on a regular basis may well mean becoming known at work, in your family or even in your political group as a pain in the ass, someone who cannot take a joke, a person who is not a good (white) team player, and it can result in some level of exclusion in social groups. We just have to remember that, while it is uncomfortable, any backlash we get as whites does not compare with the day-to-day effects of racism on people of colour. And it is better to be uncomfortable doing the right thing than to feel remorse or be guilty of doing nothing at all. Even better, responding to public acts of racism can be a good opportunity for getting to know political people of colour and deepening trust too.

By diligently taking risks, we do have to avoid the trap of thinking that being tough and dogged is enough of a strategy to be effective. It is not helpful to create an heroic anti-racist persona for ourselves that ends up casting us as lone crusaders for justice. Our methods of challenging specific acts and policies should seek to both encourage more whites making these same challenges and to open the space for the voices and actions of people of colour. As well, given that racism is persistently systemic and can easily be adapted to changing circumstances, we have to think of challenging it as a kind of baseline activity that seeks to decrease and maybe even eradicate racist hostility in certain settings, but not as a sole way to transform structures. Individual acts or isolated projects are often important but they do not a movement make.

As well, the form the intervention takes can vary with the situation. For example, regarding the anti-immigrant racism of lower income working-class whites, pointing out their privilege and calling them racist is not the most effective place to start. No one living from paycheque to paycheque feels very privileged, so arguing with someone that they are less poor, less attacked than working class people of colour may well just deepen resentment. It may be better to start with what is in common between non-white and white workers, to point out who is pulling the strings, who really gets to migrate, when and why, and the real reasons why there are not enough good jobs and housing. We need to uncover and develop the similarities in working-class conditions to show the potential we can have when we use our agency in the most constructive way, when we understand how the state and business function to pit white workers against workers of colour for ruling-class benefit. This is not about being nice or gentle; it is about being effective through showing how racism, white individuals' and the state-based forms, continues to "obscur(e) class alliances."[3] It is not enough to say that we just need to educate white workers about how they have been blaming the wrong people. People need to be responsible for their racism, whatever their conditions of life, as well as see how these two connect.

Challenging racism also means being an ally to people of colour before any overt racist act has even taken place. This can mean introducing yourself and showing interest in the one person of colour who, by some organizing feat, gets elected to the union executive of your majority-white local. Demonstrate an understanding of the structures at work and the challenges that non-white person will face within them. At the same time, it also means seeing how you and this person connect politically — just as we would with any white co-worker — to see if there are grounds there for working together on other political projects.

If we are in white-dominated political groups or workplaces, we need to acknowledge this and talk about why this is. Depending on our geographic location and the degree of social segregation in our area, such a majority may be unavoidable. But we cannot assume that there is no racism in the room if there are no people of colour or that we can comfortably see ourselves as a multiracial organization because there are two non-white people in it. We need to put the whiteness on the table, analyze and challenge it, and assess what it means in terms of what we should be doing differently and with whom we should be trying to work.

If we are white women working or volunteering in feminist non-profit agencies, we may be well on the way to this individual and collective challenging of racist acts and structures. Women of colour have led the way in pushing for an integrated anti-racism in such organizations, so a lot is happening there that is much more advanced than in many political groups. The next step, then, is for white feminists, with what they know from that setting, to take the lead on bringing that to activism and seriously contributing to anti-racist organizing for social and political change. Now that there are some good, politicized social services, we need to see that work taken out into movement building again.

Anti-Racist Organizing for Broad Social Change

Whether we find ourselves doing most of our social justice work in our neighbourhoods or in our unions, an anti-racist organizing framework follows the kinds of principles set out at the end of the last chapter. A key principle here is the core involvement and leadership of people of colour, especially women. This work also needs to be done with the understanding that *all* political work must be anti-racist work. As well, we must have a clear set of political goals, an overall strategy to get there, and a flexible set of tactics that can be applied in different situations, depending on the context and the available people. We also have to be prepared to let the strategy evolve and change as the project takes off.

While it does happen — as the WAC and NOII-Montréal examples show — it is not generally common these days to come across a group, organization or union that approaches any kind of political project in such a way. We see a lot of one-off events with little to no follow-up, as well as a lot of individually based "what-you-can-do" types of activity. And, as we have seen, we see very little white anti-racism at all. What we need is a collective, on-the-ground approach that plans where it is going and seeks to build something from each activity and event, with the transformation of our society as our ultimate goal. And here we need to accept another contradiction: while this may be our ultimate goal, it is not enough to add "anti-capitalist" to our group's basis of unity or our organization's mandate. In fact, it may be counter-productive to do so. Again, given the broader social conditions we face, in our organizing we are generally not relating to workers in the context of a broad critique of how society functions as a whole and an analysis of what we need to do to change it. Most people get involved in struggles out of dire personal need. As one WAC member commented, about getting involved in the two-year Rogers campaign and the WAC Board of Directors, "I was to-tally apolitical but this was the last straw, enough was enough."[4]

At the same time, we cannot shy away from arguments that critique capitalism, assuming that "community people" will be alienated; we shouldn't fall back onto those mainstream explanations of how our economy or society should function. For example, when government tells us that we can't raise the minimum wage because it's bad for business, we do not have to cede that terrain. We just need to be sure to put people's agency and the faults of a profit-based economic system first, while at the same time being concrete and not abstract or dogmatic.

Effective anti-racist organizing puts non-white people's agency front and centre, not in a romantic or deferential way, but based on the respectful treatment of equals. This means building trusting political relationships over the long term through being an obvious and consistent ally, and through valuing and supporting the leadership development of people of colour, especially women. Part of this is getting involved in things we may not "get." Even if our low level of awareness of the op-pressive qualities of racism or our subtle superiority complex prevent us from seeing certain political projects as a high priority or the "key piece" of "our" struggle, we can get involved in them anyway, such as when people of colour come together to organize public, political-cultural events that do not "look political" to white folks. When an opportunity is there, let's get ourselves into environments where we are the minority, do some good work, and learn about different aspects of community-based organizing at the same time. This kind of experience can help us be a white anti-racist bridge to other white-dominated political groups and settings. We have to stop expecting that if we white folks build it, then the "community people" (often code for non-whites) will come, or that the activists of colour we work with will do all the bridge work. Let's try it in reverse with a broad vision for our liberation such that, for example, women's issues are understood as those that "threaten the survival and welfare of any woman."[5]

At the same time, we do need to accept that sometimes we will work together, and at others, separately. If we build real political relationships with organizers of colour we will have the basis on which to understand when and why this must happen. One structure that was used for many years but has largely gone by the wayside in political organizing is the caucus and meeting model. As a matter of course in the meeting schedules of groups or organizations, separate spaces are created so that oppressed people get together in caucus to deal with a form of oppression from the perspective of being its target, and members of the dominant group have a meeting where, ideally, they discuss how to take on and otherwise be responsible for a form of oppression of which they are the beneficiaries. It is interesting that caucuses continue with some frequency, while meetings of people of dominant groups rarely seem to now. Sometimes there are even token attempts to blend them together so that whites do not feel excluded, a result of the ongoing white domination in the leadership of many union and community organizations. For example, a union women's conference I was at had an "Aboriginal women, women of colour and our allies" meeting, and a local co-op housing federation has had for a few years a "People of all Colours" group! At the former, only one such "ally" showed up, so what would have been a radical idea of splitting off into a separate white unionists' anti-racism meeting was not possible to propose. Clearly, oppressed people have not stopped needing a reason to meet, and members of dominant groups seem to no longer be so interested in facing each other with the tough questions about what we think and need to do. Often at conferences or in small organizations, women of colour go from caucus to caucus (for women, for people of colour, for lesbian, gay and bisexual people) while the straight white folks are sleeping in, going off to the bar or otherwise enjoying our freedom from having to deal with issues of oppression. To strategize on improving our anti-racism as part of our political work, we could look at reviving some form of those white allies meetings in our union and community settings.

Although there is no one organizing formula we can apply to all situations, the following models for organizing provide some direction on the kinds of strategies that can be developed and employed, in different contexts, with different conditions. Given that there is no template but, rather, some common methods that are effective, we can look at these models in terms of three topics: outreach, multiracial organization building, and tactics.

Outreach

Compared to the longer history of US immigrant workers' centres, the Workers' Action Centre (WAC) in Toronto is fairly new. Having started as TOFFE in 1999 with just two staff and no membership, it has made some real progress in building its base through tangible support of workers' struggles against employers and the state. One of the questions for us becomes, how does that building, that relationship development, concretely happen?

There are common denominators among WAC, US workers' centres and the NOII-Montréal outreach context and strategy. First, they are all located in larger, multiracial urban centres. This is an important point because building a multiracial organization in a Canadian city with a small population, plus an even smaller population of people of colour, is much more challenging. Second, these organizations learned to move from generalized to targeted outreach, from leafleting on street corners in communities in which you have few to no connections to figuring out how to relate to people in a more personal manner. Sarita Ahooja explains that the NOII-Montréal role of "turning up the volume" on non-status struggles was developed when they stopped leafleting for monthly assemblies and started building on connections with one or two affected people, then using community/language-specific media to get the word out to other non-status people.[6] Similarly, Emily Chan reports that WAC has shifted from doing mainly general leafleting at bus shelters or monthly drop-ins or open houses to working with the existing membership and database of people who have had support from the centre, to continue to get more people involved and expand the membership.[7] Bi-monthly orientations, monthly workers' rights workshops and regular social events are concrete, step-by-step ways to plug people into the organization. Members are also offered ongoing leadership development activities and training on workers' rights, policy, media, public speaking and workshop facilitation. Similarly, the El Paso, Texas, group Fuerza Unida, a Mexican immigrant women workers group formed in 1981, also provides concrete support to its members through leadership training and ESL classes, but also through "systemic political education."[8] I was involved for a couple of years in Toronto with a group called Justice for Workers (J4W). I got involved in this particular project as a result of the political relationships I had been developing with a few women for a number of years. Like NOII-Montréal and WAC at the start, the group itself did not have many low-wage workers. We were mainly women, both white and non-white, both unionized and non-unionized workers, working in workers' rights-related jobs, or other community organizations.[9] While the group's long-term goal was to develop a low-waged workers movement, from the fall of 2001 to late in 2004, J4W worked on a campaign to raise the Ontario minimum wage, which in 2001 was more than $3.00 an hour below the poverty line.

The group tried to have a consistent anti-racist organizing approach to this campaign in a number of ways. First of all, the campaign idea came from the workers themselves to whom we talked at subway stations, malls and community meetings during our 2000–2001 fight against the provincial government's attacks on employment standards. Second, the campaign understood that workers of colour are overrepresented in low-waged, non-unionized jobs. Third, our organizing strategy explicitly gave priority to building relationships with non-white workers in the neighbourhoods where they live and work, at times and places convenient for them, and used those meetings to carry out a campaign strategy that encouraged workers of colour to have leadership roles.

From the start, we understood outreach to be about answering the following kinds of questions: who is saying this work needs to be done, who do we already know who will want to work to get it done, and with whom do we still need to develop connections? The campaign itself came from low-wage workers. But, because society is structured this way, non-unionized workers are most often dispersed and do not come together politically or even socially as workers. Therefore, the direction we received for this campaign was based on many individuals telling us the obvious over and over again: working sixty hours a week is one problem, but making poverty wages while doing it is even worse.

In terms of who we already knew, many of us were active in feminist, anti-racist, anti-heterosexist and/or workers' rights movements for a number of years. As a result, we had some connections with immigrant and refugee advocacy networks, union organizations, community activists and neighbourhood-based organizations. Some of these were more developed than others, and some would be the basis for political relationship building and some would not.

The biggest challenge was not only to know with whom we needed to connect, but then to find a way to build consistent connections based on meaningful participation in the campaign. It was legitimate for J4W to connect with organizations and individuals and present a plan for this project. At the same time, however, we had to be flexible and scrap tactics and timelines that did not work or make sense to people. We also shared power in how we functioned so we were not just asking people to carry out a list of assigned tasks; we sought to work together, based on shared responsibility.

Other basic elements in such a conception of outreach included translating our materials into as many languages as possible and holding neighbourhood-based meetings around the city, at locations and times convenient to workers who want to be involved. Translation is a basic anti-racist organizing principle today, identified and practised by WAC, NOII-Montréal and US-based immigrant workers' centres. Moreover, in building a multiracial organization in the US context, Direct Action for Rights and Equality (DARE) found that it was not enough to translate posters and have interpreters at meetings: they had to work with the communities they were trying to build relationships with on campaigns of specific interest to them.[10]

Multiracial Organization Building
The Oregon-based Technical Assistance for Community Services (TACS) is an organization that works with all or majority white groups that want to become multiracial. The US context is different because of its population size, including the significant number of people of colour of diverse backgrounds, but their approach is reflective of anti-racist practice of the Canadian groups looked at here. They report that they focus on five main issues: 1) the recruitment process; 2) who is at the table when planning happens; 3) who is at the table when both informal and formal decision making happens; 4) how financial and other resources are allocated; and 5) how people become organizational leaders.[11]

These have been fundamental principles for WAC since it started as TOFFE in 1999. WAC has continued to develop its multiracial character as it grows, not just in total numbers, but in terms of representation at the board, committee and staff levels. Their number of staff increases in a way consistent with the communities or individual workers with whom the organization has developed a connection.

Since we were conscious of these kinds of multiracial group-building issues in J4W, when predominantly white activist and/or student-based groups wanted to get involved, we strategized together on the best way for that to happen. Inviting them to a small neighbourhood meeting of mainly working-class women of colour could have been completely counter-productive to fundamental anti-racist organizing goals. It was, of course, for the women themselves to decide but we all had in the front of our minds that these kinds of questions needed to be discussed, without waiting to see if they were raised by the community women.

We faced a challenge in J4W that one organizer in NOII-Montréal also candidly discussed. When an organizer not from the targeted oppressed group has the role of trying to facilitate the development of people's self-organization, it is often the case that folks look to that organizer to be told what to do, before stepping forward themselves. This shouldn't be surprising, given that experiencing oppression and exploitation doesn't automatically make people experts on carrying out social change. Yet, when people are at a loss and do look to the initial organizers for what to do, it is critical to keep striking that balance between leading and following, to always remember that people have agency; they just need support sometimes to get to the heart of it.[12]

As in other groups, in J4W we also needed to pay attention to expanding the original organizing group so that it not only continued to be multiracial but also included the very workers who are most affected by the campaign, so we did not have just higher-waged workers and activists representing the struggles and perspectives of the people whose lives are the target of the campaign. WAC is doing this now in a broader, systemic way as it now has a membership-based structure, and staff and members continue to work closely, both in decision making and in carrying out activities.

In J4W, we expected those of us with white or class privilege to use that to the group's advantage. My privilege allowed me to structure my life so that I could work less than full-time at a higher wage in an independent work setting, I had been able to develop a number of computer skills, and I was able to spend enough time in the South to be fluent in Spanish. These circumstances meant that I offered to do "admin tasks" or "running around" and be available for translation at events. Equally important, it did not mean I would assume I should do these things and that no one else could. Attention also has to be paid to creating the conditions in a group for sharing such responsibilities. But, as we have seen from the reality of people's lives within society's structures, we cannot change these overnight and so need to expect that some of us need to do more of some kinds of tasks than others. The NOII-Montréal group also takes the approach that it is important for more privileged people to lend their skills to enhance non-status people's self-organization.

Another part of multiracial organizing is meeting people where they are at. At WAC, when new people come to the group, they often talk about their poor wages and work conditions. This is not treated as "off topic" to the agenda. Rather, people's real life circumstances are at the heart of why this work is happening. Therefore, the group creates opportunities for figuring out how to collectively support people (for example, how they can get a paycheque from a boss withholding it or even how to get unionized).

Tactics

When there is little to no organizational base that is representative of targeted communities, the application of direct action as a tactic can end up being a kind of empty militancy, a display of radicalness that fails to acknowledge that your group is not at all in sync with its own and/or society's conditions. However, when this tactic comes from the targeted communities, when it is a thoughtful and creative part of the kind of broad movement-building strategies we have seen here, and when there is a critical mass to carry it out, it can be most effective.

Both the US-based DARE and NOII-Montréal are explicitly based on direct action in their work, and both groups seem to have had success with this. Active in Rhode Island, DARE uses "collective direct action as the primary tactic for winning community issues" as there is nothing better to empower someone than seeing a group of their angry neighbours having an affect on people in power.[13] In 1987, seventy-five kids and parents marched into the Parks Commissioner's office to demand decent playgrounds for the children. As a result, the campaign spread city-wide and after six or seven years, ten playgrounds had been renovated and 200 vacant lots cleaned up in low-income neighbourhoods.

Although the bigger political project is different, the NOII-Montréal application of direct action tactics seems to come from the same place as DARE: the communities targeted. Along with groups like the Action Committee of Non-Status Algerians, NOII has organized confrontational, vibrant demonstrations and occupations of the Immigration Minister's office to fight deportations. In June 2005, Solidarity Without Borders, of which NOII is part, organized a one-week march from Montréal to Ottawa as part of the struggle of immigrants for life and dignity. The four basic demands of the Solidarity Without Borders network are: the regularization of all non-status people in Canada; an end to deportations; an end to detentions; and the abolition of security certificates.[14]

As we have seen, WAC employs a variety of tactics depending on the situation. They file official complaints, do press conferences, carry out popular education and leadership training and hold spirited demonstrations. They also did a "bad boss bus tour" in 2004. The demos are powerful not only because of the creative mix of popular theatre, music and public speaking: they are also powerful for their active representation of the multiracial character of the group and its political project. In campaign planning meetings, members are actively involved in assessing the use of different tactics. For example, if a petition is suggested, how will it be used to best push politicians and continue to build the involvement of more people? Can it be used at both meetings with MPPs and to build for demonstrations? Or, will it be useful at all?

What is interesting about exploring the J4W example is that, while it shares a lot of characteristics with the other groups and organizations mentioned — in terms of political understanding of and approach to outreach and the broad goals of social change through multiracial, anti-racist organizing — it is not what anyone could call a successful project. After three years of applying the methods outlined above, the group was still one of activists rather than community people turned activists. There were, of course, hopeful moments and the work of the few community people who did get involved was valuable. We had one community event in the Jane-Finch neighbourhood of Toronto to which more than 150 people came. Two women in our group from that neighbourhood gave an inspiring talk on the importance of the campaign and of local mobilization.

Yet, our promising moments did not evolve into a movement. Realizing that activists cannot be stand-ins for the grassroots, J4W members agreed in 2004 to end the campaign. This experience is one of many that shows how even the best political approach does not guarantee success. At the end of the day, even after a few years of applying an evolving strategy, the group was left to deal with the social conditions within which it was working. For example, the target group was low-waged workers, a group opposite in composition to that of the Quebec Algerians. Low-waged workers are not a specific cultural or social community located in any particular area of Toronto, and so the challenges for regularly connecting with a consistent group of people are significant, as are the possibilities of self-organization. Nor are they being faced with an imminent life or death threat; the attack on low-waged workers is more one of low intensity, precarious-work warfare. As a result, a minimum-wage campaign was an obvious positive project to people; it wasn't obvious, though, what their immediate relationship to this medium- or long-term project ought to be. As well, during that campaign, not the least of our problems was the challenge of getting active involvement from the organizations of unionized labour. Who would think that a campaign to improve workers' rights would be led by a community group rather than by unions?

This points to the ongoing problem of the separation between community and union organizing. Some of the larger unions fund specific types of community projects through social justice funds, but it is quite a political process to get access to the limited money available. The odd, small, left-wing local will support community-based campaigns through involvement, funds or in-kind donations, but they are far too rare indeed.

Anti-Racist Organizing in Unions

Better and broader anti-racist organizing also needs unionized labour to make some serious changes in the way it functions. While a few unions have some good educational programs, relatively few rank-and-file people have access to them, and many unions do little to nothing in the way of ongoing anti-racism work. The very fact that workers of colour are underrepresented in unions shows racism within those organizations. Yet, to effectively organize workers of colour, unions must be committed to structural changes that open up access to financial resources, take direction from progressive rank-and-file unionists, integrate workers of colour into the union in a meaningful way, make serious implementation of anti-racist education and policies a priority, and actively develop union-community joint projects. Following are some important considerations for anti-racist union organizing, specifically for unionizing workers of colour.[15]

Unions cannot wait for workers to call them. They need to go out to where the workers are, using a well-thought-out strategy. Part of a willingness to do this means that expanding the dues base by giving priority to larger and/or higher paid workplaces cannot be the primary consideration. This requires union organizations to strategize on how to organize homeworkers, temp agency workers and other precarious workers. As well, unions must not give up fighting for migrant farm workers' rights to unionize. The structural realities of limiting legislation and the nature of precarious work can make this a significant challenge, as people have shorter term work and generally cannot take their union certification with them from job to job.

Given these kinds of challenges, it becomes even more important for unions to build a support base well before any unionizing drive begins. Community connections and involvement are fundamentally important. A union cannot just pick a target company, round up their white, English-speaking organizers and go leaflet at the company gates. This does not work for the union or the workers. This can mean meeting with community-based organizations and/or political groups that have day-to-day connections with workers who are structured into certain kinds of work. For example, the Philippine Solidarity Group has been a critical community connection for getting to know home-care workers in Toronto.

Another strategy that has many benefits is the development of union-funded workers' centres. There are almost none in this country. In addition to WAC, another centre that has been around since the late 1990s is the Winnipeg Workers' Organizing and Resource Centre (WORC). The former gets project-specific funding from some unions while WORC receives core funding from the Canadian Union of Postal Workers (CUPW). Non-unionized workers drop in to WORC and get support for workplace complaints and find out how to unionize, and the centre also provides free meeting space and other supports for various community projects. Yet, it has only one part-time staff person and

WORC seems to be lacking in a serious race consciousness, so evidence of an anti-racist, community-based approach to their work is difficult to see. Unions would benefit from funding workers' centres with explicit anti-racist organizing mandates as such centres can be an important pre-organizing forum.

As we saw with the community-based organizing of WAC and NOII-Montréal, person-to-person contact with workers through one-on-one and small group, home-based, organizing meetings is much more effective than general leafleting. Prior to this, all materials need to be translated into the languages workers speak. Radio stations and programming in various languages can also promote unionizing.

Another important consideration is more than knowing what connections there are in communities of colour; it is recruiting, hiring and training organizers who are local community members and who speak the language of the workers. That means not just training people to be organizers once in a while; it means having active union drives and always available training. And these organizers must be centrally involved in developing the organizing strategies. As well, unions must be flexible and provide, for example, child care and transportation support to organizers with family and community commitments. It is also important to have actual rank-and-file union members involved in the organizing campaign. This is critical for integration of new members after a successful drive and also assists with strategizing about effective pressure tactics to use in the workplace during a drive. It is hoped that CUPE's recent member-organizer training will receive enough ongoing official support to allow those unionists to apply their knowledge.

Once a local is organized, efforts cannot stop there. Because union work is often compartmentalized into organizing, service provision and education, often when a drive is finished the organizers who have been the main connection to the workers disappear and white staff representatives come out of nowhere. So this whole approach has to happen through union structures. At the same time, when unions combine the roles of organizer, educator and service-provider, they have to contribute enough resources so that one super-person is not expected to do all this in seventy hours a week.

Finally, workers need to have meaningful involvement and real leadership in their unions. Our unions need to stop holding on to their top-heavy structures, to open up and make real democratic participation possible. This serious problem of union structure is a tangible social condition that needs a lot of work to change.

If this is what unions as a whole need to do, what does this mean for the average unionized worker? It means they have to push, from the membership of their locals, for this kind of change. They need to get local members on-side, get an executive elected that will move on these ideas, and seek its own connections with non-unionized workers of colour, then push the union to support its efforts to organize. We are a long way from seeing these steps carried out but we will not get there without strategizing about how to make co-ordinated efforts.

Conclusion

We have got to collectively figure out how to seriously build a movement again. It is not enough to be enraged at the international legitimating of yet another bombing or occupation, or at how more and more families of colour are doubling up in two-bedroom apartments because decreasing wages do not pay for increasing rents, or at how the Chief of Toronto Police continues to deny that Black men are targeted by the cops, or at how more Arabs and West Asians are deported to certain danger. The rage we feel must guide us into actively challenging the historical and ongoing roots of those injustices as we also look to people of colour for direction and instruction on how best to move forward, together when we can, separately when we must.

As explored in these past five chapters, taking responsibility and direction for anti-racism by white leftists requires more than just a bit of a balancing act. While as individuals we need to grasp the full complexity of our agency, we must at the same time see the limits of taking personal responsibility for the historical length and breadth of racism as a social relation. As well, as white leftists step forward, individually when we must, collectively when we can, we have to be willing not only to take risks and explore new territory but to face being wrong sometimes too. Taking such risks is easier when we let go of remorse-based anti-racism and all the confusion and odd behaviour it has bred. We don't have to feel, at worst, fascinated or foolish about our privilege and whiteness, and, at best, simply stuck and unsure what to do. Instead, we can see whiteness and its associated privilege in relation to ourselves as individuals and our lives in this time and place, at the same time as we see the development and reality of white supremacy and racism as historical, systemic phenomena that are beyond our own fault or our simple will to overhaul in any one group, project or moment. Getting rid of the remorse-based perspective provides fewer opportunities for the "great white hope" approach that is a byproduct of both white supremacy and white guilt. It makes it easier to figure out just what taking direction means, in different situations.

When we look for direction, we do not need to be completely deferential and remain silent; we ought instead to be actively listening and contributing to political discussions with people of colour about how to develop our collective strategies. This becomes easier as people get to know us and trust starts to develop, a key foundation of any successful political relationship. Through working with people, we learn to follow and lead at the same time. To do this well takes time. Some feminist and other community organizations have taken the time to do this kind of work, internally and within their own networks. Now they must externalize this political activity again, getting involved once more in broader movement building.

Again, there is no one formula for anti-racist organizing. What I have suggested here is meant to sketch what is possible and necessary. In these models we can also find some inspiration and hope. When one person's back wages are won, when one deportation is stopped, these are indeed important successes because they are about individual human lives. Yet, when determined self-organization combined with effective solidarity results in many more wages being paid or many more migrants obtaining status, these are victories that may also mean that we are on the right track to building something broader.

Even if we are in a place in Canada, where such hopeful multiracial organizing is taking place, we still the face the question, how do we generalize these successes? Various types of social conditions make this a daunting challenge, not the least of which is the increasingly privatized and commodifying form of international capitalism that is more ruthless and effective than ever at sucking increasing profits out of our labour while its structures alienate and isolate us from each other. The very nature of precarious work — whether that means having three part-time, underpaid jobs or one overworked, seasonal and still underpaid migrant worker's job — ensures workers are either not together long enough for co-ordinated action or are structurally separated so as to seriously hinder the development of a shared sense of social location. The material and the ideological impacts of neo-liberalism go hand in hand: working people are generally making less of a living for doing more and more work, but the implications about which side of the fence we should be on and who we should want there with us ensure that we generally do not see that basis for class solidarity. Instead, at best, white folks are to stick to a superficial business-like multiculturalist approach to relating to people of colour; at worst, we are supposed to fear migrants of colour as terrorists or "illegals" out to steal our jobs.

Taking serious responsibility also means that leftists must solidly challenge our various sectarian and self-righteous ways. This is in terms not only of many far leftists' approach to developing more and more small groups, with endlessly more particular versions of what specific program or analysis will carry us forward; it's also in relation to the heavy moral tone of some anti-oppression leftists about white privilege and what whites need to do about it. The former brand of sectarianism isolates us more from a working class already highly fragmented and stratified by race, gender and neo-liberalism; the latter type just digs the remorse in deeper, making developing trusting, mutual political relationships more difficult.

I spent most of the fall of 2001 in an inspired rage. The rage was about the US attack on Afghanistan and the ratcheting-up of domestic racism. The inspiration came from the multiracial organizing that, although short-lived, blossomed in response to it. I remember one discussion-oriented meeting I attended at which there were a lot of white folks. I was uncharacteristically unable to control my anger at all when I spoke, that rage gushing forth as I said, "It's f—'n time we white folks stepped up to the plate!" Now, where that plate is and how to find it aren't easy questions to answer. But, I still have that sharp feeling that we simply can no longer let it go on, as more "security laws" get put in place, as more and more migrants are restricted or permitted only temporary access. Rights are being reduced and racism is on the rise. So we've got to get on it.

There are white people willing to step up to the plate. I think there are many of us. This past year I met thirty of them while facilitating two Toronto Women's Bookstore workshops based on the material in this book. In each session, fifteen different women, mostly white, came together with a candour, an openness and a willingness to explore new ideas and analysis that will move white anti-racism forward. They ranged in age from twenty to over sixty; they came from unions and university; they were teachers, social workers, community workers and activists. And they courageously challenged themselves and each other to (re)examine racism and white privilege, both street-level and structural, and to tackle the complexity of how it keeps getting perpetuated, our (white) involvement in it, and what we could be doing differently and better. I suppose, in these times, this is where my inspiration comes from regarding white anti-racism.

Moving forward, then, requires not only the balancing act of taking responsibility/taking direction. It also requires balancing hopefulness and inspiration with a thoughtful assessment of conditions and possibilities. It feels, here in my lifetime, like it's high time we get down to it. And I will not say I hope that we can do that because, at some point, we simply must.

Notes

Chapter One

1 This detailed background comes from Mary Gellatly's Toronto Coaltion Against Racism (TCAR) archives. It was the police who publicly identified the attacks as "racially motivated."

2 I got involved in TCAR in 1997, during its denouement, when there were only a handful of active members left trying to continue with some immigrant and refugee rights work, through educational forums. The last activity was a fundraiser to pay off the group's debts. For years to come, it was a little joke in some Toronto activist circles that many who feel connected with anti-racist activism will at some point say "oh yeah, I was involved with TCAR," even if they only went to one demo or just read a pamphlet. This not uncommon desire to demonstrate a connection to the coalition speaks to its importance at the time as a force in the anti-racism movement. As well, the reference to the challenge of the project is not just about the formidable state and street-level attacks the group was fighting; it's also about the internal difficulties when left groups form coalitions: the grappling with differences in perspective on politics, overall strategy and use and application of tactics.

3 In a September 9, 2005, e-mail, Hamid Sodeifi went on to say, "It was also very militant. The anger and militancy on the face of the participants was undeniable. At one point, near Sherbourne Avenue, a skinhead with ample stupidity decided to come out of his hole to challenge the crowd. He was very lucky that the cops were there to save his sorry ass. Despite the palpable anger, the demonstration was also very disciplined. ... There are probably only half a dozen of such powerful examples for each one of us (given the unfortunate times in which we live) to reminisce about."

4 A line from Billy Bragg's "I Don't Need This Pressure Ron," on *Preaching to the Converted*. Permission for use courtesy of Crysalis Music.

5 To understand Canada as an imperialist power, we need only to look at the diverse and lucrative activities of Canadian multinational corporations (MNC) abroad and the expanding presence of Canadian banks in the political South. MNC activity ranges from telecommunications to forestry to shoe manufacturing. And these Canadian businesses are quite healthy in relation to US ones: between 1994 and 2001, 384 more US businesses were bought by Canadian ones than the reverse, at a cost of $46 billion to Canadian capitalists. With investors enjoying a dividend surplus of $3.5 billion in

2000, it is easy to say that Canadian imperialism is alive and well. See David McNally, "War and Imperialism, Canadian Style," *New Socialist* 41 (2003).

6 Becky Thompson, *A Promise and A Way of Life: White Anti-Racist Activism* (Minneapolis: University of Minnesota Press, 2001), xv and 150.

7 William Aal, "Moving from Guilt to Action: Antiracist Organizing and the Concept of 'Whiteness' for Activism and the Academy," in *The Making and UnMaking of Whiteness*, ed. Birgit Brander Rasmussen, Eric Klinenburg, Irene J. Nexica and Matt Wray (London: Duke University Press, 2001), 295.

8 Paul Rubio, "Crossover Dreams: The 'Exceptional White' in Popular Culture," in *Race Traitor*, ed. Noel Ignatiev and John Garvey (New York: Routledge, 1996), 151.

9 "By not talking about it much (we) can make (ourselves) believe (we) are not racist ... and everything is okay. (We) might avoid making contact with (people) of colour for this reason; talking to them might make it obvious that (we) have attitudes that (we) have to change or else talking to them brings up (our) fear about what they're thinking about (us), so it's easier not to talk. Besides there's the question of what to talk about. (We're) not comfortable talking to them about racism ... because it emphasizes the differences yet (we) can't stop thinking about it or worrying about it or feeling afraid and guilty around them." Vancouver Rape Relief, "Privilege," workshop hand-out.

10 Aal, "Moving," 305.

11 Ibid., 304.

12 Thompson, *Promise*, 79.

13 Mullard in F. Henry and C. Tator, "State Policy and Practice as Racialized Discourse: Multiculturalism, the Charter, and Employment Equity," in *Race and Ethnic Relations in Canada*, ed. Peter S. Li, sec. ed. (Toronto: Oxford University Press, 1999), 98.

14 Hoon Lee, "Building Class Solidarity Across Racial Lines: Korean-American Workers in Los Angeles," in *Beyond Identity Politics: Emerging Social Justice Movements in Communities of Color*, ed. John Anner (Boston: South End Press, 1996).

15 For comments on the rigidity and specificity of racism, see (respectively) Stuart Hall, "Race, Culture and Communications: Looking Backward and Forward at Cultural Studies," in *Rethinking Marxism* 5, 1 (Spring 1992): 13; and Nahla Abdo, "Race Gender and Politics: The Struggle of Arab Women in Canada," in *And Still We Rise: Feminist Political Mobilizing in Contemporary Canada*, ed. Linda Carty (Toronto: Women's Press, 1993), 79.

16 Anne Bishop, "Becoming an Ally," workshop handout from Heads Up Collective, 1994. See also Anne Bishop's second edition of *Becoming an Ally* (Halifax: Fernwood Publishing, 2002).

Chapter 2

1 James R. Barrett and David Roediger, "How White People Became White," in *Critical Whiteness Studies: Looking Behind the Mirror*, ed. Richard Delgado and Jean Stefancic (Philadelphia: Temple University Press, 1997), 592.

2 Michael Oni, "(E)racism: Emerging Practice of Antiracist Organization," in *The*

Making and UnMaking of Whiteness, ed. Rasmussen, Klinenburg, Nexica and Wray, 279.

3 For a detailed generally history of racism, see Robert Miles, *Racism* (London: Routledge, 1989).

4 For a linking of race and class see Linda Carty and Dionne Brand," 'Visible Minority' Women: A Creation of the Canadian State," in *Returning the Gaze: Essays on Racism, Feminism and Politics*, ed. Himani Bannerji (Toronto: Sister Vision Press, 1993).

5 See Tania Das Gupta for a look at how stereotypes are "fixed ideas about people, usually based on insufficient or erroneous information," in *Racism and Paid Work* (Toronto: Garamond, 1996), 10.

6 Himani Bannerji, "Introducing Racism: Notes Towards an Anti-Racist Feminism," *Resources for Feminist Research* 16, 1 (March 1987): 10-12.

7 Henry and Tator, "State Policy," 91.

8 Michael Ornstein, *Ethno-Racial Inequality in Toronto: An Analysis of the 1996 Census Data* (York University: Institute for Social Research, March 2002).

9 Patricia Hill Collins, *Black Feminist Thought: Knowledge, Consciousness and the Politics of Empowerment*, sec. ed. (New York: Routledge, 2000), 69.

10 See Himani Bannerji's comments on commonsense racism in "Introducing Racism," and "On the Dark Side of the Nation: Politics of Multiculturalism and the State of 'Canada,'" *Journal of Canadian Studies* 31, 3 (Fall 1996).

11 And, given that the production and purchase of goods and services are for the primary purpose of making profit, most people have to sell their labour power to employers. The employers' interest in this relationship is to keep wages as low as possible to keep the profit margin as high as they can. The workers selling their labour are doing so just to get access to purchasing the goods and services on the market.

12 See Ellen Woods's explanation in "Capitalism," *New Socialist* 37 (August-September 2002): 14-15.

13 Das Gupta, "Racism," 3.

14 For a full discussion of class composition and re-composition see David Camfield, "Reorienting Class Analysis: Working Classes as Historical Formations," *Science and Society* 68, 4 (Winter 2004).

15 For a detailed analysis of white privilege see Peggy McIntosh, "White Privilege. Unpacking the Invisible Knapsack," *Independent School* (Winter 1990): 31-36.

16 Agnes Calliste and George J. Sefa Dei, "Anti-Racist Feminism: A Conclusion to a Beginning," in *Anti-Racist Feminism: Critical Race and Gender Studies*, ed. Agnes Calliste and George J. Sefa Dei (Halifax: Fernwood. 2000), 31.

17 For comments on this see, Bannerji, "On the Dark Side."

18 Peggy McIntosh developed this graphic inventory of invisible social advantages of whiteness: "White privilege is like an invisible weightless knapsack of special provisions, maps, passports, code books, visas, clothes, tools and blank checks" ("White Privilege," 31).

19 See Miles, *Racism*, 190, and Roxanna Ng, "Sexism, Racism, Canadian Nationalism," in *Returning the Gaze: Essays on Racism, Feminism and Politics*, ed. Bannerji.

20 See Bannerji's "On the Dark Side," 104.

21 Carty and Brand say, therefore, "state policy around issues of race, class or sex can be characterized as a policy of containment and control" ("Visible Minority," 229).

22 Enakshi Dua, "Canadian Anti-Racist Feminist Thought: Scratching the Surface of Racism," in *Scratching the Surface: Canadian Anti-Racist Feminist Thought*, ed. Enakshi Dua and Angela Robertson (Toronto: Women's Press, 1999), 26.

Chapter 3

1 From Bannerji, "On the Dark Side," 107.

2 For a longer discussion of the ushering in of the "TINA" era, see Daniel Singer, *Whose Millennium? Theirs or Ours?* (New York: Monthly Review Press, 1999).

3 See James Walker, *"Race," Rights and the Law in the Supreme Court of Canada* (Toronto: The Osgoode Society UILU Press Canada, 1997), 13.

4 For an exhaustive historical study of whiteness in the US see Theodore Allen, *The Invention of the White Race*, volume one (London: Verso, 1994).

5 Miles, *Racism*, 11. Much of what I present on the history of othering is from Miles' detailed analysis.

6 "A white/black contrast expressed a complex set of additional meanings ... such as good/evil, pure/diabolical, spiritual/carnal and Christ/Satan." Ibid., 16.

7 See Maria Castagna and George Dei for further remarks: "The racist belief that white people were to rule the world (Manifest Destiny) ... (was) a powerful colonizing tool." "A Historical Overview of the Application of the Race Concept in Social Practice," in *Anti-Racist Feminism*, ed. Calliste and Dei, 24.

8 See Allen, *Invention*.

9 For a discussion of the relationship between racism and capitalism see David McNally, *Another World Is Possible* (Winnipeg: Arbeiter Ring Publishing, 2002), 104.

10 "It was common practice for masters to baptize their slaves so they might have 'salvation'; such conversion rarely resulted in emancipation." Sylvia Hamilton, "Naming Names, Naming Ourselves: A Survey of Early Black Women in Nova Scotia," in *We're Rooted and They Can't Pull Us Up*, ed. Peggy Bristow, Dionne Brand, Linda Carty, Afua P. Cooper, Sylvia Hamilton and Adrienne Shadd (Toronto: University of Toronto Press, 1994), 17.

11 Cecilia Morgan, "Turning Strangers into Sisters? Missionaries and Colonization in Upper Canada," in *Sisters or Stangers? Immigrant, Ethnic, and Racialized Women in Canadian History*, ed. Marlene Epp, Franca Iacovetta, Frances Swyripa (Toronto: University of Toronto Press, 2004).

12 Miles, *Racism*, 25.

13 While it is a somewhat overly intellectual history of race, see a useful contribution by Kenan Malik, *The Meaning of Race: Race, History and Culture in Western Society* (New York: New York University Press, 1996).

14 Miles, *Racism*, 76.

15 See Castagna and Dei, "Historical Overview," as well as Peter S. Li, "The Multicultural Debate," in *Race and Ethnic Relations in Canada*, ed. Peter S. Li, sec. ed. (Toronto:

Oxford University Press, 1999).

16 See Malik, "Meaning of Race," 47, for how he summarizes this connection: "the discourse of scientific racism ... holds that there is one world but that it is inhabited by different types of humanity, whereas the discourse of culture holds that there is one type of humanity but that it inhabits different worlds."

17 Linda Carty, "The Discourse of Empire and the Social Construction of Gender," in *Scratching the Surface*, ed. Dua and Robertson, 35.

18 Allen, *Invention*.

19 McNally, *Another World*, 109.

20 For a discussion of functionalism, see Derek Sayer, *The Violence of Abstraction* (New York: Basil Blackwell, 1987).

21 Miles, *Racism*, 40.

22 Walker, "Race," 247.

23 See Patience Elaba-Idemudia, "Challenges Confronting African Immigrant Women in the Canadian Workforce," in *Anti-Racist Feminism*, ed. Calliste and Dei, 9.

24 Sarah Carter, *Aboriginal People and Colonizers of Western Canada to 1900* (Toronto: University of Toronto Press, 1999), 55.

25 Miles, *Racism*, 26.

26 For a detailed account of empires' different histories of imperialist expansion, see Ellen Meiksins Woods, *Empire of Capital* (London: Verso, 2003).

27 Ibid., 89.

28 Carter, *Aboriginal People*, 40, 42.

29 Daiva Stasiulis and Radha Jhappan, "The Fractious Politics of a Settler Society: Canada, "in *Unsettling Settler Societies: Articulations of Gender, Race, Ethnicity and Class*, ed. Daiva Stasiulis and Nira Yuval-Davis (London: Sage, 1995), 101.

30 Carter, *Aboriginal People*, 51-52.

31 Deborah Lee Simmon, "Against Capital: The Political Economy of Aboriginal Resistance in Canada," PhD dissertation, York University, 1995, 197.

32 Donna Kahenrakwas Goodleaf, "Under Military Occupation: Indigenous Women, State Violence and Community Resistance," in *And Still We Rise*, ed. Carty, 226.

33 Stasiulis and Jhappan, "Fractious Politics," 102. See Carter, *Aboriginal People*, 37, where she says that it has been estimated that the Aboriginal population in what is now Canada was two million in the late fifteenth century, whereas in the early twentieth century, it was just over 125,000 people, or 7% of the earlier size.

34 For example, Montagnais-Naskapi women were often forced through abuse by their Aboriginal male partners to convert to Christianity, after the latter had themselves been pressured by the colonizers. See Winona Stevenson, "Colonialism and First Nations Women in Canada," in *Scratching the Surface*, ed. Dua and Robertson.

35 Bannerji, "On the Dark Side," 106.

36 Clearly, this continues with First Nations today with the state's ongoing determination to marginalize, exclude and repress Aboriginal people, stalling on land claims negotiations (as in the racist referendum of spring 2002 in BC), denying Aboriginal inherent rights to resource access (as in the active bond between the Canadian government and white fishers in Burnt Church, NS, to trample Native rights to food and livelihood) and in how both European-origin ruling classes and other whites came together to violently repress the 1990 Kanehsatake uprising.

37 Stasiulus and Jhappan, "Fractious Politics," 102.

38 Stevenson, "Colonialism," 54.

39 Carter, *Aboriginal People*, 57. Her use of the term "Western Canada," while it pre-dates Confederation, is descriptive of the territory from northwestern Ontario west to BC.

40 Ibid., 59. Sarah Carter details the painful case of one Aboriginal woman who lost her husband, family, home, community and her class position as a result of her British husband's abandoning her and marrying a white English woman.

41 See Adele Perry's detailed study, *On the Edge of Empire: Gender, Race and The Making of British Columbia, 1849-1871* (Toronto: University of Toronto Press, 2001).

42 One result was the militancy of Métis people such as Louis Riel, still often described in school history lessons as a traitor rather than a legitimate nationalist leader of his time.

43 Perry, *On the Edge*, 51. On page 111 Perry also eloquently comments on the failure of social and spatial segregation, as "Imperial visions of orderly white communities" kept running into "the rough and ready mixed-race social practice of the colony."

44 Stasiulus and Jhappan, "Fractious Politics," 104.

45 But not just any labour force was wanted. As we will see later, even with pro-settlement policies in place, many non-white workers who were allowed to migrate as temporary workers were not allowed to sponsor their families.

46 From the Website http://friends of grassy narrows.com.

47 Goodleaf, "Military Occupation," 227.

48 Stasiulus and Jhappan, "Fractious Politics," 101.

49 Perry, *On the Edge*, 52.

50 Ibid., 63.

51 Ibid., 64.

52 That is, given all the reasons looked at previously: the strong role of women, the egalitarian nature of many Indigenous societies, the diametrically opposed value systems, and the strength of their ability to resist domination, militarily, socially, economically and culturally.

53 For reference to Canadian slavery, see Adrienne Shadd, "Institutionalized Racism and Canadian History: Notes of a Black Canadian," in *Racism in Canada*, ed. Ormond McKague (Saskatoon: Fifth House Publishing, 1991); and Linda Carty, "African Canadian Women and the State: 'Labour Only Please,'" in *We're Rooted and They Can't Pull Us Up*, ed. Bristow, Brand, Carty, Cooper, Hamilton and Shadd. As Sylvia Hamilton also states, "As early as 1605, from her first arrival in Nova Scotia, the Black woman has had to struggle for survival. She has had to battle slavery, servitude, sexual and racial discrimination, and ridicule," in "Naming Names," 13.

54 See Stasiulis and Jhappan, "Fractious Politics," 108, and also Hamilton, "Naming

Names," for a discussion of Black migration to Canada.

55 As Dionne Brand reports, "Black women of the time had inherited not only the burdensome legacy of a labour force stratified by race and gender but also a social milieu steeped in racial hatred." "'We Weren't Allowed To Go Into Factory Until Hitler Started the War': The 1920s and the 1940s," in *We're Rooted and They Can't Pull Us Up*, ed. Bristow, Brand, Carty, Cooper, Hamilton and Shadd, 172.

56 Shadd, "Institutionalized Racism," 3.

57 See PASST (Provincial Association of Social Studies Teachers), Quebec Board of Black Educators, Ministere de L'Education, *Some Missing Pages: The Black Community in the History of Quebec and Canada*, 1996. See also Hamilton, "Naming Names," 27 and Carty, "African Canadian Women."

58 Stasiulis and Jhappan, "Fractious Politics."

59 Lorna McLean and Marilyn Barber, "In Search of Comfort and Independence: Irish Immigrant Servants Encounter the Courts, Jails and Asylums in Nineteenth-Century Ontario," in *Sisters or Stangers? Immigrant, Ethnic, and Racialized Women in Canadian History*, ed. Epp, Iacovetta and Swyripa, 133-160.

60 Ibid., 109. Also Enakshi Dua, "'The Hindu Women's Question': Canadian Nation Building and the Social Construction of Gender for South-Asian Canadian Women," in *Anti-Racist Feminism*, ed. Calliste and Dei.

61 Ibid., 141.

62 Miles, *Racism*, 112.

63 Malik, *Meaning of Race*, 116.

64 Carty, "Discourse of Empire," 38.

65 Castagna and Dei, "Historical Overview," 31.

66 F. Henry and Carol Tator, "State Policy," 192.

67 As Bannerji relates, this mythology masks "the same Canada as a post-conquest capitalist state, economically dependent on an imperialist United States and politically implicated in English and US imperialist enterprises, with some designs of its own." See "On the Dark Side," 115.

68 Stasiulus and Jhappan, "Fractious Politics," 107.

69 See Henry and Tator ("State Policy," 92), as well as Bannerji ("On the Dark Side") and Simmons (*Against Capital*) on this topic.

70 As Ng states, "Immigration policies have always been designed to meet and regulate the needs of the Canadian economy while, as much as possible, preserving Canada as a predominantly white nation." Roxanna Ng, *The Politics of Community Services: Immigrant Women, Class and State* (Toronto: Garamond Press, 1988), 16.

71 Stasiulus and Jhappan, "Fractious Politics."

72 Bruce R. Shepard, "Plain Racism: The Reaction Against Oklahoma Black Immigration to the Canadian Plains," in *Racism in Canada*, ed. Ormond McKague, 19.

73 For a detailed look at what Chinese migrants faced in BC, see Gillian Creese's "Organizing Against Racism in the Workplace: Chinese Workers in Vancouver Before the Second World War," in *Racism in Canada*, ed. Ormond McKague.

74 Castagna and Dei, "Historical Overview," 34.

75 Roxanna Ng, "Sexism, Racism, Canadian Nationalism," 234.

76 Stasiulus and Jhappan, "Fractious Politics," 112.

77 Gillian Creese relates how the "white labour movement excluded Asians from their trade unions, boycotted businesses employing Asians, pressed for legislation to protect jobs for white men and were at the forefront of the movement to end further Asian migration." See "Organizing Against Racism," 36.

78 From Canadian Broadcasting Corporation (CBC), News item, Sunday, May 19, 2002.

79 Dua, "'Hindu Women's Question,'" 59.

80 This section draws on Ruth A. Frager's *Sweatshop Strife: Class, Ethnicity and Gender in the Jewish Labour Movement of Toronto 1900–1939* (Toronto: University of Toronto Press, 1992).

81 Ibid., 44.

82 See Karen Brodkin's *How Jews Became White Folks and What that Says About Race in America* (New Jersey: Rutgers University Press, 1998). While the focus is on the US and there were differences in both the broader context and the patterns of Jewish migration, we can draw similar conclusions about the essential absence of structural anti-Semitism in Canada today.

83 Brand, "'We Weren't Allowed,'" 174.

84 Ibid., 181

85 Ibid., 182.

86 Stasiulus and Jhappan, "Fractious Politics," 117.

87 Miles, *Racism*, 124.

88 For examples see Ng, *Community Services*, and Stasiulus and Jhappan, "Fractious Politics."

89 See Tania Das Gupta's "Unravelling the Web of History," in *Resources for Feminist Research* 16, 1 (March 1987): 13-14.

90 See Brand, "We Weren't Allowed," 189 and also Carty, "African Canadian Women."

91 From Das Gupta, "Unravelling the Web," 13.

92 See Shadd, "Institutionalized Racism," 4.

93 Donna Baines and Nandita Sharma, "Migrant Workers as Non-Citizens," in *Studies in Political Economy* 69 (2002): 90.

94 Tania Das Gupta, "The Politics of Multiculturalism: Immigrant Women and the Canadian State," in *Scratching the Surface*, ed. Dua and Robertson, 196.

95 From Chris Ramsaroop and Sonia Singh, personal conversation, September 16, 2002.

96 Baines and Sharma, "Migrant Workers," 90.

97 Elaba-Idemudia, "Challenges Confronting African Immigrant Women." Also, Sedef Arat-Koc, "Gender and Race In 'Non-discriminatory' Immigration Policies in Canada," in *Scratching the Surface*, ed. Dua and Robertson.

98 Stasiuslus and Jhappan, "Fractious Politics," 118.

99 See Arat-Koc, "Gender and Race," 209.

100 Stasiuslus and Jhappan, "Fractious Politics," 118.

101 Himani Bannerji, *Thinking Through: Essays on Feminism, Marxism and Anti-Racism* (Toronto: Women's Press, 1995), 31.

102 Canadian Labour Congress, *Women's Work: A Report by the Canadian Labour Congress*, March 5, 1997.

103 Agnes Calliste reports that in the late '80s and '90s, "black nurses were over-represented in low-paid chronic care institutions/wards and on night shifts, and were often assigned heavy patient load and duties involving mostly menial work—'black women's work.'" Agnes Calliste, "Women of 'Exceptional Merit': Immigration of Caribbean Nurses to Canada," *Canadian Journal of Women and the Law* 6, 1 (1993): 85-102.

104 Das Gupta, "Politics of Multiculturalism."

105 Thompson, *Promise*, 185.

106 Carty and Brand, "Visible Minority," 214.

107 Miles, *Racism*, 51.

108 Dua, "'Hindu Women's Question,'" 69.

109 Christina Gabriel, "Restructuring at the Margins," in *Scratching the Surface*, ed. Dua and Robertson, 145.

110 Carty, "Discourse of Empire," 41.

111 Kathryne Mitchell, "In Whose Interest? Transnational Capital and the Production of Multiculturalism in Canada," in *Global/Local Cultural Production of the Transnational Imaginary*, ed. Rob Wilson and Wimal Dissanauche (Durham and London: Duke University Press, 1999).

112 Ibid., 223.

113 Canadian Broadcasting Corporation (CBC), news item, August 11, 2002.

114 Heads Up Collective, "A Heads Up on the Immigration and Refugee Protection Act: Bill C-31," *Community Action Notes* 4 (December 1, 2001).

115 See the Canadian Arab Federation's "Provisions in Bill C-18 Must Be Removed," press release, Toronto, February 10, 2003. The Bill died after second reading because of an election call.

116 Yasmeen Abu-Laban and Christina Gabriel, *Selling Diversity: Immigration, Multiculturalism, Employment Equity, and Globalization* (Peterborough: Broadview Press, 2003).

117 Bannerji, "On the Dark Side," 117, 118.

118 M. Nourbese Phillips, "Why Multiculturalism Can't End Racism," in *Frontiers: Essays and Writings on Racism in Canada* (Toronto: The Mercury Press, 1992), 185.

119 Das Gupta, "Politics of Multiculturalism," 187.

120 Li, "Multicultural Debate," 149.

121 Arat-Koc, "Gender and Race."

122 The example of France was developed through my June 3, 2005, conversation with Raghu Krishnan, a Canadian leftist who spent a number of years in France and was active in Canadian anti-racist organizing in the '80s and '90s. Such a comparison needs much more research if one really wants to answer the question 'is Canada less racist than other Western nations?' This is not the point here. The comparison is introduced to indicate that multiculturalism may well have a mitigating effect on racism — or it may entrench it. The particular historical circumstances of each country are critical to this comparison. For example, France's long history of secularism dates back to the French revolution's fight to break the power of the church. This background has likely as much to do with the controversial measures to ban the hijab (and other religious symbols of other religions) from public schools. French society has not been racially or culturally divided on this issue, nor has it only been the right wing that supports the law and the left that opposes it. In fact, it was a far-right leader, Nicolas Sarkozy (Minister of the Interior), who carried through in late 2002 a kind of official multiculturalism, seeking and getting the support of some Muslim groups for a Muslim council. While Jews and Christians had developed historical official institutional relationships with the state, Muslims have not had that opportunity. As such, the institution of a "representative Islamic council" might be said to be a form of multiculturalism through religious pluralism. Apparently, while proposed first by more left-wing ministers of the interior in 1990 and 1997, much of the left outside government and many of the communities who would be the supposed beneficiaries of such a council opposed it as an opportunistic, pseudo-multiculturalism designed to give the electorate "the feeling of balance" as Sarkozy prepares to win the 2007 elections. This kind of "multicultural effort" has one effect of conflating one's country of origin (or that of one's parents or grandparents) with religion: not all people connected to Maghreb countries are Muslim and in France many are not, but this council is often seen as representing all people of Maghreb origin. As well, there is quite a range of expressions of Islam among Muslims. The left asks, and rightly so, why not focus on high unemployment of the Maghreb-origin French population and the war on Iraq, rather than on religion? See also www.Politis.Fr/article391.html and /article551.html.

123 Malik, "Meaning of Race," 30.

124 Li summarises in one paragraph the two-pronged origins of multiculturalism. See "Race and Ethnicity," 151-152.

125 For example, there are many people of colour from Britain with Anglo-Saxon heritage but the fact that they are not white overrides those origins and so their social location tends to be more outsider than insider.

126 B. Singh Bolaria and Peter S. Li, *Racial Oppression in Canada*, sec. ed. (Toronto: Garamond Press, 1988).

127 Bannerji, "On the Dark Side," 117.

128 Das Gupta, "Politics of Multiculturalism," 187.

129 Das Gupta states, "The ruling class, in particular state institutions, can absorb some demands of the 'grassroots' in order to neutralize popular resistance. It would rather go through some form of equity reform ... than be made vulnerable to its core social relations." Ibid., 194.

130 Abu-Laban and Gabriel, *Selling Diversity*, 111.

131 Stasiulus and Jhappan, "Fractious Politics," 123.

132 Abu-Laban and Gabriel, *Selling Diversity*, 113.

133 Bannerji, "On the Dark Side," 123.

134 Mohanty says, "'managing diversity' is a 'semantic gem' that suggests that 'diversity' (a euphemism for people of colour) will be out of control unless it is managed." Quoted in Thompson, *Promise*, 311.

135 Hoon Lee, "Building Class Solidarity," 49.

136 Karen Hurley, Personal conversation, November 1, 2002.

Chapter 4

1 Allen, *Invention*.

2 Ibid., 16.

3 Thomas Dunk, "Racism, Ethnic Prejudice, Whiteness and the Working Class," in *Racism and Social Inequality in Canada*, ed. Vic Satzewich (Toronto: Thompson Publishing, 1998), 218.

4 Miles, *Racism*, 81.

5 Bannerji, *Thinking Through*, 35.

6 Malik, *Meaning of Race*, 251-252.

7 "New York City police officers, having identified an African immigrant as a Black man killed him on the spot. There was no dialogue or negotiation, just as enslavement was no matter for dialogue or negotiation between owners and their property," In Barbara J. Fields, "Whiteness, Racism and Identity," *International Labor and Working-Class History* 60 (Fall 2001): 49.

8 Alma Estable, Mechthild Meyer, and Gordon Pon, *Teach Me to Thunder: A Training Manual for Anti-Racism Training*, Handout 15 (Ottawa: Canadian Labour Congress and Gentium Consulting, 1997) 11.

9 Malik, *Meaning of Race*, 154.

10 John Garvey, *Race Traitor*, ed. Ignatiev and Garvey, 129.

11 Bannerji, *Thinking Through*, 35.

12 That is, the rejection of some and the taking on of other specific forms of culture as important for abolition of white supremacy. For example, getting into hip-hop is seen as an anti-racist, cultural cross-over activity.

13 Paul Rubio, "Crossover Dreams: The 'Exceptional White' in Popular Culture," in *Race Traitor*, ed. Ignatiev and Garvey, 51.

14 Salim Washington, "Responses to Crossover Dreams," in *Race Traitor*, ed. Ignatiev and Garvey, 165.

15 Bannerji, *Thinking Through*, 72.

16 Castagna and Dei,"Historical Overview," 30.

17 Christine E. Sleeter, "White Silence, White Solidarity," in *Race Traitor*, ed. Ignatiev and Garvey, 260.

18 What this can mean for non-white women in this context is, "Our 'difference' then is not simply a matter of 'diversities,' which are being suppressed arbitrarily, but a way of noting and muting at the same time fundamental social contradictions and antagonisms." Bannerji, *Thinking Through*, 72.

19 Rassmussen, Klinenburg, Nexica, and Wary, ed. *The Making and Unmaking of Whiteness*, 287.

20 Malik, *Meaning of Race*, 253.

21 Mitchell, "In Whose Interest?," 220.

22 "Once we saw colonization as destruction of economies and drain of wealth; now we see its crimes as being those of robberies of representation." Bannerji, *Thinking Through*, 36.

23 Julia Sudbury, *Other Kinds of Dreams: Black Women's Organizations and the Politics of Transformation* (London: Routledge, 1998), 150.

24 Fields, "Whiteness," 51.

25 Das Gupta, *Racism and Paid Work*, 3.

26 Bannerji, *Thinking Through*, 31.

27 Miles, *Racism*, 90.

28 While "historically some white groups were racialized, there was still a hierarchy of privilege based on skin colour." Castagna and Dei, "Historical Overview," 32.

29 Fields, "Whiteness," 50.

30 Morton Weinfeld and Lori A. Wilkinson, "Immigration, Diversity and Minority Communities," in *Race and Ethnic Relations in Canada*, ed. Peter S. Li, 58.

31 Creese, "Organizing Against Racism."

32 Rassmussen, Klinenburg, Nexica, and Wary, ed., *The Making and Unmaking of Whiteness*, 267.

33 From a May 19, 2005, telephone interview with Sarita Ahooja, an organizer with NOII-Montréal.

34 As Ahooja and I discussed, it's easy to talk about racism when people of colour are around but when they aren't what do you do?

35 Francis Lee Ansley, "Stirring the Ashes: Race, Class and the Future of Civil Rights Scholarship," in *Critical Whiteness Studies*, ed. Delgado and Stefancic, 592.

36 From an interview with Dave Brophy, member of Winnipeg Friends of Grassy Narrows, April 26, 2005, and a personal conversation on August 23, 2005. He went on to say, "After a certain point, I think, to remain in the mode of strictly listening takes on an almost colonial extractive dynamic."

37 From the Colours of Resistance Website. http://www.tao.ca/~colours/. Accessed January 5, 2003.

38 Brophy, personal conversation, 2005.

39 As one Armenian Iranian woman has put it, "In many ways we feel like we have been left out in your organizing, we feel like instead of asking our opinion or ways that our community can be helped, many activists have come in and told us what we need to do and how we need to give a press conference and where we need to go, what protest to show up at and what meetings to attend ... I don't think our people should be used as a sort of sideshow." From Shiva, "Why are White Activists Ignoring Middle Eastern People?" in Heads Up Collective, *Community Action Notes* (January

13, 2002).

40 Anti-Racist Action at www.antiracistaction.ca/pou.html.

41 Thompson, *Promise*, 49.

42 See the Canadian Labour Congress, *No Easy Recipe: Building the Diversity and Strength of the Labour Movement*, Feminist Organizing Models CLC Women's Symposium, November 1–3 1998.

43 In the education system alone, "white women are overwhelmingly today's social workers and teachers ... (as) these professions are saturated with imperial longing to save, civilize or educate unfortunate others." Sherene Razack, "Your Place or Mine? Transnational Feminist Collaboration," in *Anti-Racist Feminism: Critical Race and Gender Studies*, ed. Calliste and Dei, 46.

44 That is, in name if not in function. The NOII groups across Canada seem to vary in how interconnected they are in terms of their shared projects. There is no national decision-making body. They have the same political goals and mandate but they appear to differ greatly in how they implement these. The Vancouver-based Website (http://noii-van-resist.ca) says that NOII "is in full confrontation with Canadian colonial border policies, denouncing and taking action to combat racial profiling of immigrants and refugees, detention and deportation policies, and wage-slave conditions of migrant workers and non-status people."

45 Nandita Sharma, "Open the Borders!" *New Socialist* 37 (August-September, 2002): 6-8.

46 Ahooja, telephone interview.

47 For example, these include the Action Committee of Non-Status Algerians, organized a few years ago, as well as Colombian, Palestinian and South Asian migrants.

48 "Non-status" is the progressive term used to describe people here without the documents required by the Canadian government. Rather than saying someone is "illegal," this use of "non-status" neutralizes the social and political judgement implied by "illegal." "Non-status" and the opposite term, "status," then function to be descriptive yet demonstrative of the power imbalance between these two externally-imposed social positions.

49 Ahooja, telephone interview.

50 From a personal conversation with David Camfield, NOII-Winnipeg member, May 20, 2005.

51 From an e-mail communication with Harsha, a NOII-Vancouver activist, May 15, 2005. Their Website is http://noii-van-resist.ca.

52 I was an active, founding member of this group in Toronto for a number of months.

53 In a few words, the source of the political dissatisfaction was the 'inside' groups' well-meaning (and even courageous, to a certain extent) pseudo-therapeutic approach to framing a multiracial response to racism. It was brave in intention but using therapeutic techniques for community organizing was off the mark politically.

54 I say 'was' because, while Heads Up is still nominally together, the public presence they had from late 2001 to 2003 is essentially non-existent in 2005.

55 From an e-mail conversation with WAC staff member Emily Chan, June 3,

2005.

56 From an interview with former Rogers worker and current WAC board member Zainab Taiyeb, June 3, 2005.

57 Ibid.

58 From an interview with Dave Brophy, member of Winnipeg Friends of Grassy Narrows, April 26, 2005, and a personal conversation on August 23, 2005.

59 Ibid.

60 Ibid.

61 Colours of Resistance at http://www.tao.ca/~colours/. Accessed January 5, 2003.

62 Anti-Racist Action at www.antiracistaction.ca/pou.html. Accessed 2002.

63 Alex Callinicos, "Race and Class," *International Socialism*, 55 (Summer 1992): 4.

64 Ibid., 15.

65 Ibid., 20.

66 Sue Findlay, "Problematizing Privilege: Another Look at the Representation of Women in Feminist Practice," in *And Still We Rise,* ed. Carty.

67 Enakshi Dua, "Canadian Anti-Racist Feminist Thought," 17.

68 Beverly Bain and Naomi Binder Wall, "The Integrative Feminist Anti-Racism Anti-Oppression Model to Facilitating Support Groups," WCREC Workshop Series, May 2002, 2.

69 Dua, "Canadian Anti-Racist Feminist Thought," 10.

70 David Harvey, *The Condition of Postmodernity* (Cambridge, Mass.: Blackwell, 1990), 7.

71 Ali Rattansi, "Just Framing: Ethnicities and Racisms in a 'Postmodern' Framework," in *Social Postmodernism: Beyond Identity Politics,* ed. Linda Nicholson, Steven Seidman, and Jeffrey C. Alexander (Cambridge: Cambridge University Press, 1995), 250.

72 Malik, *Meaning of Race,* 219.

73 Rattansi, "Just Framing," 251.

74 Ibid., 253.

75 Castagna and Dei, "Historical Overview," 31.

76 Vic Satzewich, "The Political Economy of Race and Ethnicity," in *Race and Ethnic Relations in Canada,* ed. Peter S. Li.

77 Kathleen Neal Cleaver, "The Anti-Democratic Power of Whiteness," in *Critical Whiteness Studies,* ed. Delgado and Stefancic, 161.

78 Dunk, "Racism, Ethnic Prejudice," 217.

79 James R. Barrett and David Roediger, "How White People Became White," in *Critical Whiteness Studies,* ed. Delgado and Stefancic, 402.

80 "The state of whiteness was approached gradually and controversially. The authority of the state itself both smoothed and complicated that approach." Ibid., 405.

81 Satzewich, "Political Economy," 322-323.

82 Dunk, "Racism, Ethnic Prejudice," 219.

83 Ibid., 212.

84 Allen, *Invention*, 159.

85 Dunk goes on to say: "In a situation where political rights are defined on the basis of race, an ideological appeal to Irish workers on racial rather than class lines worked because workers gained something by identifying with other 'whites' as 'whites' rather than with workers as workers." "Racism, Ethnic Prejudice," 213.

86 Allen, *Invention*, 185.

87 Ibid.

88 Satzewich, "Political Economy," 323.

89 Noel Ignatiev and John Garvey, "Introduction: A Beginning," in *Race Traitor*, ed. Ignatiev and Garvey, 2.

90 Noel Ignatiev, "Treason to Whiteness is Loyalty to Humanity," in *Critical Whiteness Studies*, ed. Delgado and Stefancic, 607.

91 "The abolitionists maintain ... that people were not favored socially because they were white; rather they were defined as 'white' because they were favored." Ignatiev and Garvey, "Introduction," 10.

92 That is, a culture characterized by "ravenous materialism, competitive individualism, and a way of living characterized by putting acquisition of possessions above humanity. One need not be of European descent to participate in such a way of living, but it is a way of living that people of European descent constructed and sell, and one that we are persistently socialized to identify with and support." Sleeter, "White Silence," 264.

93 Deena Ladd, Personal conversation, October 15, 2002.

94 Estable, Meyer, and Pon, *Teach Me To Thunder*, 7.

95 In terms of the size and composition of this union, the PSAC Website (http://www.psac-afpc.org) states, "Our membership is diverse and growing. While many of our 150,000 members work for the federal government or agencies as immigration officers, fisheries officers, food inspectors, customs officers and the like, an increasing number of PSAC members work in the private sector in women's shelters, universities, security agencies and casinos. In the North, the PSAC represents most unionized workers employed by the governments of the Yukon, Nunavut and the Northwest Territories and some municipalities."

96 From a conversation with Carol Wall, August 21, 2005, currently a PSAC negotiator but also the woman of colour who managed—against all odds and against the many attempts of various arms of union bureacracies to prevent it—to get 37% of the CLC delegates vote in a recent election that saw Ken Georgetti win again.

97 As it says on the national Website, www.cupe.ca, "The Canadian Union of Public Employees (CUPE) is Canada's largest union. With more than half a million members across Canada, CUPE represents workers in health care, education, municipalities, libraries, universities, social services, public utilities, transportation, emergency services and airlines. A strong and democratic union, CUPE is committed to improving the quality of life for workers in Canada ... CUPE members are service-providers, white-collar workers, technicians, labourers, skilled trades people and professionals. More than half of CUPE members are women. About one-third are part-time workers."

98 At http://www.cupe.ca/www/EqualityRacism/4174 is the following union position on racism and why it needs to be fought:

"Eliminating racism in our workplaces and in our world! The facts:

- CUPE workers of colour and Aboriginal members tend to be concentrated in lower paying occupations with poorer working conditions. Our workplaces should not be segregated this way!

- Discriminatory hiring practices are one of the ways workers of colour and Aboriginal workers are shut out of better paying unionized workplaces.

- This kind of systemic racism is worldwide and its impact in our Canadian workplaces is very real and devastating.

- As privatization and restructuring lead the assault on better-paying public sector jobs, workers of colour and Aboriginal workers are particularly vulnerable because last-hired, first-fired policies erode their gains.

- While the populations of our communities change and become more diverse, the face of our workforce is not keeping pace with these changes.

Challenging racism in our workplaces means:

- Reaching out to all CUPE members, welcoming everyone's participation and ensuring that all union activities reflect the diversity of our membership.

- Putting anti-racism on the bargaining agenda and negotiating clear and specific contract language for racism-free workplaces.

- Educating our members, co-workers and communities by exploding the myths that sustain racism.

- Organizing workers of colour and Aboriginal workers because unionized workers have better wages and working conditions.

- Building links with community groups fighting for equality.

- Strengthening our union solidarity. When one of us cannot be exploited, none of us can."

99 This is in British Columbia, April 3–8 2005, the Solidarity and Racial Justice Workshop.

100 From an e-mail from Stephanie Ross, September 9, 2005, whose Ph.D. dissertation was on CUPE. She also said, "Overall, I would characterize the activism around anti-racism as focused on representation of workers of colour in elected leadership positions, human rights conferences designed to bring together equity activists from many communities, as well as education of members via diversity workshops."

101 From an e-mail from CUPE 3903 member Neil Braganza, August 22, 2005.

102 From a personal conversation with CUPE 79 activist Julia Barnett, August 26, 2005.

103 See Susan Ursel and Cindy Wilkey, *Human Rights: Collective Agreements, Union Obligations and Liabilities* (Toronto: Ontario Federation of Labour, 1999).

104 See the Canadian Labour Congress, *Challenging Racism.*

105 Ibid., 27, 43.

Chapter 5

1 The partial regularization program was beneficial to those with families, jobs and formal education; that is, those of a better class position. From an e-mail conversation with Sarita Ahooja, September 4, 2005.

2 There was much debate both during and after this experience about whether to "go public" about the travails. Most women did not want to, presumably to avoid a more generalized experience of what happened in the group itself. That is why I do not say the name of the group here.

3 Brand, "Black Women and Work," 95.

4 From a June 3, 2005, interview with Zainab Taiyeb.

5 Sudbury, *Other Kinds of Dreams*, 216.

6 From an interview with Sarita Ahooja, May 18, 2005.

7 From an e-mail communication from Emily Chan, WAC staff member, June 3, 2005.

8 Miriam Ching Yoon Lowes, *Sweatshop Warriors: Immigrant Women Workers Take on the Global Factory* (Boston: South End Press, 2001), 86.

9 TOFFE was one organization that was quite involved in this campaign, through staff involvement and providing meeting space.

10 Anner, ed., *Beyond Identity Politics*.

11 Ibid., pg. 163.

12 Ahooja, interview, 2005.

13 Anner, ed., *Beyond Identity Politics*, 17.

14 See http://noii-van.resist.ca.

15 Canadian Labour Congress, *No Easy Recipe*. Also, input from a personal conversation with Deena Ladd, October 15, 2002.

Bibliography

Aal, William. "Moving from Guilt to Action: Antiracist Organizing and the Concept of 'Whiteness' for Activism and the Academy." In *The Making and UnMaking of Whiteness*. Birgit Brander Rasmussen, Eric Klinenburg, Irene J. Nexica and Matt Wray, ed. Durham and London: Duke University Press, 2001.

Abdo, Nahla. "Race, Gender and Politics: The Struggle of Arab Women in Canada." In *And Still We Rise: Feminist Political Mobilizing in Contemporary Canada*. Linda Carty, ed. Toronto: Women's Press, 1993.

Abu-Laban, Yasmeen, and Christina Gabriel. *Selling Diversity: Immigration, Multiculturalism, Employment Equity, and Globalization*. Peterborough: Broadview Press, 2003.

Allen, Theodore. *The Invention of the White Race*. Volume One. London: Verso, 1994.

Anner, John. "Introduction." In *Beyond Identity Politics: Emerging Social Justice Movements in Communities of Color*. John Anner, ed. Boston: South End Press, 1996.

Ansley, Francis Lee. "Stirring the Ashes: Race, Class and the Future of Civil Rights Scholarship." In *Critical Whiteness Studies: Looking Behind the Mirror*. Richard Delgado and Jean Stefancic, ed. Philadelphia: Temple University Press. 1997.

Anti-Racist Action. www.antiracistaction.ca/pou.html. 2002.

Arat-Koc, Sedef. "Gender and Race in 'Non-discriminatory' Immigration Policies in Canada." In *Scratching the Surface: Canadian Anti-Racist Feminist Thought*. Enakshi Dua and Angela Robertson, ed. Toronto: Women's Press, 1999.

Bain, Beverly, and Naomi Binder Wall. "The Integrative Feminist Anti-Racism Anti-Oppression Model to Facilitating Support Groups." WCREC Workshop Series. May 2002.

Baines, Donna, and Nandita Sharma. "Migrant Workers as Non-Citizens." *Studies in Political Economy* 69 (Autumn 2002).

Balagoon, Kuwasi. *When Race Burns Class*. Toronto: Arm the Spirit and Solidarity, 2000.

Bannerji, Himani. *The Dark Side of the Nation: Essays on Multiculturalism, Nationalism and Gender*. Toronto: Canadian Scholar's Press, 2000.

————. "Introducing Racism: Notes Towards an Anti-Racist Feminism." *Resources for Feminist Research* 16, 1 (March 1987).

————. "On the Dark Side of the Nation: Politics of Multiculturalism and the State of 'Canada.'" *Journal of Canadian Studies* 31, 3 (Fall 1996).

————. *Thinking Through: Essays on Feminism, Marxism and Anti-Racism*. Toronto: Women's Press, 1995.

Barrett, James R. and David Roediger. "How White People Became White." In *Critical Whiteness Studies: Looking Behind the Mirror*. Richard Delgado and Jean Stefancic, ed. Philadelphia: Temple University Press, 1997.

Bishop, Anne. "Becoming an Ally." Workshop Handout from Heads Up Collective, 1994.

Bolaria, B. Singh, and Peter S. Li. *Racial Oppression in Canada*. Second edition. Toronto: Garamond Press, 1988.

Brand, Dionne. "Black Women and Work: The Impact of Racially Constructed Gender Roles on the Sexual Division of Labour." In *Scratching the Surface: Canadian Anti-Racist Feminist Thought*. Enakshi Dua and Angela Robertson, ed. Toronto: Women's Press. 1999.

————. "'We Weren't Allowed To Go Into Factory Until Hitler Started the War': The 1920s and the 1940s." In *We're Rooted and They Can't Pull Us Up*. Peggy Bristow, Dionne Brand, Linda Carty, Afua P. Cooper, Sylvia Hamilton, and Adrienne Shadd, ed. Toronto: University of Toronto Press, 1994.

Callinicos, Alex. "Race and Class." *International Socialism* 55 (Summer 1992).

Calliste, Agnes. "Women of 'Exceptional Merit': Immigration of Caribbean Nurses to Canada." *Canadian Journal of Women and the Law* 6, 1 (1993).

Calliste, Agnes and George J. Sefa Dei. "Anti-Racist Feminism: A Conclusion to a Beginning." In *Anti-Racist Feminism: Critical Race and Gender Studies*. Agnes Calliste and George J. Sefa Dei, ed. Halifax: Fernwood, 2000.

Camfield, David. "Reorienting Class Analysis: Working Classes as Historical Formations." *Science and Society* 68, 4 (Winter 2004).

Canadian Arab Federation. "Provisions in Bill C-18 Must Be Removed." Press Release. Toronto, February 10, 2003.

Canadian Broadcasting Corporation (CBC). News item. August 11, 2002.

————. News item. Sunday, May 19, 2002.

Canadian Labour Congress. *No Easy Recipe: Building the Diversity and Strength of the Labour Movement*. Feminist Organizing Models CLC Women's Symposium. November 1-3, 1998.

————. *Challenging Racism: Going Beyond Recommendations*. Report of the CLC National Anti-Racism Task Force. October 1997.

————. *Women's Work: A Report by the Canadian Labour Congress*. March 5, 1997.

Carroll, William K, ed. *Organizing Dissent*. Second edition. Toronto: Garamond Press, 1997.

Carter, Sarah. *Aboriginal People and Colonizers of Western Canada to 1900*. Toronto: University of Toronto Press, 1999.

Carty, Linda. "African Canadian Women and the State": 'Labour Only Please.'" In *We're Rooted and They Can't Pull Us Up*. Peggy Bristow, Dionne Brand, Linda Carty, Afua P. Cooper, Sylvia Hamilton, and Adrienne Shadd, ed. Toronto: University of Toronto Press, 1994.

————. "The Discourse of Empire and the Social Construction of Gender." In *Scratching the Surface: Canadian Anti-Racist Feminist Thought*. Enakshi Dua and Angela Robertson, ed. Toronto: Women's Press, 1999.

Carty, Linda, and Dionne Brand. "'Visible Minority' Women: A Creation of the Canadian State." In *Returning the Gaze: Essays on Racism, Feminism and Politics*. Himani Bannerji, ed. Toronto: Sister Vision Press, 1993.

Castagna, Maria, and George J. Sefa Dei. "A Historical Overview of the Application of the Race Concept in Social Practice." In *Anti-Racist Feminism: Critical Race and Gender Studies*. Agnes Calliste and George J. Sefa Dei, ed. Halifax: Fernwood, 2000.

Cleaver, Kathleen Neal. "The Anti-Democratic Power of Whiteness." In *Critical Whiteness Studies: Looking Behind the Mirror*. Richard Delgado and Jean Stefancic, ed. Philadelphia: Temple University Press, 1997.

Colours of Resistance. http://www.tao.ca/~colours/. January 5, 2003.

Creese, Gillian. "Organizing Against Racism in the Workplace: Chinese Workers in Vancouver Before the Second World War." In *Racism in Canada*. Ormond McKague, ed. Saskatoon: Fifth House Publishing, 1991.

Das Gupta, Tania. "The Politics of Multiculturalism: Immigrant Women and the Canadian State." In *Scratching the Surface: Canadian Anti-Racist Feminist Thought*. Enakshi Dua and Angela Robertson, ed. Toronto: Women's Press, 1999.

————. *Racism and Paid Work*. Toronto: Garamond, 1996.

————. "Unravelling the Web of History." *Resources for Feminist Research* 16, 1 (March 1987).

Dua, Enakshi. "Canadian Anti-Racist Feminist Thought: Scratching the Surface of Racism." In *Scratching the Surface: Canadian Anti-Racist Feminist Thought*. Enakshi Dua and Angela Robertson, ed. Toronto: Women's Press, 1999.

————. "'The Hindu Women's Question': Canadian Nation Building and the Social Construction of Gender for South-Asian Canadian Women." In *Anti-Racist Feminism: Critical Race and Gender Studies*. Agnes Calliste and George J. Sefa Dei, ed. Halifax: Fernwood, 2000.

Dunk, Thomas. "Racism, Ethnic Prejudice, Whiteness and the Working Class." In *Racism and Social Inequality in Canada*. Vic Satzewich, ed. Toronto: Thompson Publishing, 1998.

Elaba-Idemudia, Patience. "Challenges Confronting African Immigrant Women in the Canadian Workforce ." In *Anti-Racist Feminism: Critical Race and Gender Studies*. Agnes Calliste and George J. Sefa Dei, ed. Halifax: Fernwood, 2000.

Estable, Alma, Mechthild Meyer, and Gordon Pon. *Teach Me to Thunder: A Training Manual for Anti-Racism Training*. Ottawa: Canadian Labour Congress and Gentium Consulting, 1997.

Fields, Barbara J. "Whiteness, Racism and Identity." *International Labor and Working-Class History* 60 (Fall 2001).

Findlay, Sue. "Problematizing Privilege: Another Look at the Representation of Women in Feminist Practice." In *And Still We Rise: Feminist Political Mobilizing in Contemporary Canada*. Linda Carty, ed. Toronto: Women' s Press, 1993.

Frager, Ruth A. *Sweatshop Strife: Class, Ethnicity and Gender in the Jewish Labour Movement of Toronto 1900-1939*. Toronto: University of Toronto Press, 1992.

Gabriel, Christina. "Restructuring at the Margins." In *Scratching the Surface: Canadian Anti-Racist Feminist Thought*. Enakshi Dua and Angela Robertson, ed. Toronto: Women's Press. 1999.

Goodleaf, Donna Kahenrakwas. "Under Military Occupation: Indigenous Women, State Violence and Community Resistance." In *And Still We Rise: Feminist Political Mobilizing in Contemporary Canada*. Linda Carty, ed. Toronto: Women' s Press, 1993.

Hall, Stuart. "Race, Culture and Communications: Looking Backward and Forward at Cultural Studies." *Rethinking Marxism* 5, 1 (Spring 1992).

Hamilton, Sylvia. "Naming Names, Naming Ourselves: A Survey of Early Black Women in Nova Scotia." In *We're Rooted and They Can't Pull Us Up*. Peggy Bristow, Dionne Brand, Linda Carty, Afua P. Cooper, Sylvia Hamilton, and Adrienne Shadd, ed. Toronto: University of Toronto Press, 1994.

Harvey, David. *The Condition of Postmodernity*. Cambridge, Mass.: Blackwell, 1990.

Heads Up Collective. "A Heads Up on the Immigration and Refugee Protection Act: Bill C-31." *Community Action Notes*. Toronto. Issue 4, December 1, 2001.

Henry, F., and Carol Tator. "State Policy and Practice as Racialized Discourse: Multiculturalism, the Charter, and Employment Equity." In *Race and Ethnic Relations in Canada*. Peter S. Li, ed. Second edition. Toronto: Oxford University Press, 1999.

Hill, Daniel G. *The Freedom Seekers: Blacks in Early Canada*. Agincourt: The Book Society of Canada Ltd., 1981.

Hill Collins, Patricia. *Black Feminist Thought: Knowledge, Consciousness and the Politics of Empowerment*. Second edition. New York: Routledge, 2000.

Hurley, Karen. Personal conversation. November 1, 2002.

Ignatiev, Noel. "Treason to Whiteness Is Loyalty to Humanity." In *Critical Whiteness Studies: Looking Behind the Mirror*. Richard Delgado and Jean Stefancic, ed. Philadelphia: Temple University Press, 1997.

Ignatiev, Noel and John Garvey. "Introduction: A Beginning." In *Race Traitor*. Noel Ignatiev and John Garvey, ed. New York: Routledge, 1996.

Kivel, Paul. *Uprooting Racism: How White People Can Work for Racial Justice*. Gabriola Island: New Society Publishers, 2002.

Ladd , Deena. Personal conversation. October 15, 2002.

Lee, Hoon. "Building Class Solidarity Across Racial Lines: Korean-American Workers in Los Angeles." In *Beyond Identity Politics: Emerging Social Justice Movements in Communities of Color*. John Anner, ed. Boston: South End Press, 1996.

Li, Peter S. "Race and Ethnicity." In *Race and Ethnic Relations in Canada*. Peter S. Li, ed. Second edition. Toronto: Oxford University Press, 1999.

————. "The Multicultural Debate." In *Race and Ethnic Relations in Canada*. Peter S. Li, ed. Second edition. Toronto: Oxford University Press, 1999.

Lowe, Miriam Ching Yoon. *Sweatshop Warriors: Immigrant Women Workers Take on the Global Factory*. Boston: South End Press, 2001.

Malik, Kenan. *The Meaning of Race: Race, History and Culture in Western Society*. New York: New York University Press, 1996.

McIntosh, Peggy. "White Privilege. Unpacking the Invisible Knapsack." *Independent School* (Winter, 1990).

McLean, Lorna, and Marilyn Barber. "In Search of Comfort and Independence: Irish Immigrant Servants Encounter the Courts, Jails and Asylums in Nineteenth-Century Ontario." In *Sisters or Stangers? Immigrant, Ethnic, and Racialized Women in Canadian History*. Marlene Epp, Franca Iacovetta, and Frances Swyripa, ed. Toronto: University of Toronto Press, 2004.

McNally, David. *Another World Is Possible*. Winnipeg: Arbeiter Ring Publishing, 2002.

Miles, Robert. *Racism*. London: Routledge, 1989.

Mitchell, Kathryne. "In Whose Interest? Transnational Capital and the Production of Multiculturalism in Canada." In *Global/Local Cultural Production of the Transnational Imaginary*. Rob Wilson and Wimal Dissanauche, ed. Durham and London: Duke University Press, 1999.

Morgan, Cecilia. "Turning Strangers into Sisters? Missionaries and Colonization in Upper Canada." In *Sisters or Stangers? Immigrant, Ethnic, and Racialized Women in Canadian History*. Marlene Epp, Franca Iacovetta, and Frances Swyripa, ed. Toronto: University of Toronto Press, 2004.

Morrison, Tony. "Playing in the Dark: Whiteness and the Literary Imagination." In *Critical Whiteness Studies: Looking Behind the Mirror*. Richard Delgado and Jean Stefancic, ed. Philadelphia: Temple University Press, 1997.

Mukherjee, Arun. "A House Divided: Women of Colour and American Feminist Theory." In *Challenging Times: The Women's Movement in Canada and the United States*. Constance Backhouse and David H. Flaherty, ed. Montreal and Kingston: McGill-Queen's University Press, 1992.

Nadeau, Mary-Jo. "Who is Canadian Now? Feminism and the Politics of Nation After September 11." *Atlantis 27*, 1 (2002).

Ng, Roxanna. *The Politics of Community Services: Immigrant Women, Class and State*. Toronto: Garamond Press, 1988.

————. "Sexism, Racism, Canadian Nationalism." In *Returning the Gaze: Essays on Racism, Feminism and Politics*. Himani Bannerji, ed. Toronto: Sister Vision Press, 1993.

Oni, Michael. "(E)racism: Emerging Practice of Antiracist Organization." In *The Making and UnMaking of Whiteness*. Birgit Brander Rasmussen, Eric Klinenburg, Irene J. Nexica and Matt Wray, ed. London and Durham: Duke University Press, 2001.

Ornstein, Michael. *Ethno-Racial Inequality in Toronto: An Analysis of the 1996 Census Data*. York University: Institute for Social Research, March 2002.

PASST (Provincial Association of Social Studies Teachers), Quebec Board of Black Educators, Ministere de L'Education. *Some Missing Pages: The Black Community in the History of Quebec and Canada*. Gouvernement du Quebec, 1996.

Perry, Adele. *On the Edge of Empire: Gender, Race and The Making of British Columbia, 1849-1871*. Toronto: University of Toronto Press, 2001.

Phillips, M. Nourbese. "Why Multiculturalism Can't End Racism." In *Frontiers: Essays and Writings on Racism in Canada*. Toronto: The Mercury Press, 1992.

Ramsaroop, Chris, and Sonia Singh. Personal conversation. September 16, 2002.

Rassmussen, Birgit Brander, Eric Klinenburg, Irene J. Nexica and Matt Wary, ed. *The Making and Unmaking of Whiteness*. London and Durham: Duke University Press, 2001.

Rattansi, Ali. "Just Framing: Ethnicities and Racisms in a 'Postmodern' Framework." In *Social Postmodernism: Beyond Identity Politics*. Linda Nicholson, Steven Seidman, and Jeffrey C. Alexander, ed. Cambridge: Cambridge University Press, 1995.

Razack, Sherene. "Your Place or Mine? Transnational Feminist Collaboration." In *Anti-Racist Feminism: Critical Race and Gender Studies*. Agnes Calliste and George J. Sefa Dei, ed. Halifax: Fernwood, 2000.

Rubio, Paul. "Crossover Dreams: The 'Exceptional White' in Popular Culture." In *Race Traitor*. Noel Ignatiev and John Garvey, ed. New York: Routledge, 1996.

Satzewich, Vic. "The Political Economy of Race and Ethnicity." In *Race and Ethnic Relations in Canada*. Peter S. Li, ed. Second edition. Toronto: Oxford University Press, 1999.

Sayer, Derek. *The Violence of Abstraction*. New York: Basil Blackwell, 1987.

Shadd, Adrienne. "Institutionalized Racism and Canadian History: Notes of a Black Canadian." In *Racism in Canada*. Ormond McKague, ed. Saskatoon: Fifth House Publishing, 1991.

Sharma, Nandita. "Open the Borders!" *New Socialist* 37 (August-September, 2002).

Shepard, Bruce R. "Plain Racism: The Reaction Against Oklahoma Black Immigration to the Canadian Plains." In *Racism in Canada*. Ormond McKague, ed. Saskatoon: Fifth House Publishing, 1991.

Shiva. "Why are White Activists Ignoring Middle Eastern People?" *Community Action Notes*. Heads Up Collective. Toronto. January 13, 2002.

Simmons, Deborah Lee. *Against Capital: The Political Economy of Aboriginal Resistance in Canada*. PhD Dissertation, York University. 1995.

Singer, Daniel. *Whose Millennium? Theirs or Ours?* New York: Monthly Review Press, 1999.

Sleeter, Christine E. "White Silence, White Solidarity." In *Race Traitor*. Noel Ignatiev and John Garvey, ed. New York: Routledge, 1996.

Stasiulus, Daiva, and Radha Jhappan. "The Fractious Politics of a Settler Society: Canada." In *Unsettling Settler Societies: Articulations of Gender, Race, Ethnicity and Class*. Daiva Stasiulus and Nira Yuval-Davis, ed. London: Sage, 1995.

Stevenson, Winona. "Colonialism and First Nations Women in Canada." In *Scratching the Surface: Canadian Anti-Racist Feminist Thought*. Enakshi Dua and Angela Robertson, ed. Toronto: Women's Press, 1999.

Sudbury, Julia. *Other Kinds of Dreams: Black Women's Organizations and the Politics of Transformation.* London: Routledge, 1998.

Thobani, Sunera. "War Frenzy." *Atlantis* 27, 1 (2002).
Thompson, Becky. *A Promise and A Way of Life: White Anti-Racist Activism.* Minneapolis: University of Minnesota Press, 2001.

Ursel, Susan, and Cindy Wilkey. *Human Rights: Collective Agreements, Union Obligations and Liabilities.* Toronto: Ontario Federation of Labour, 1999.

Vancouver Rape Relief. "Privilege." Workshop hand-out.

Walker, James. *'Race,' Rights and the Law in the Supreme Court of Canada.* Toronto: The Osgoode Society UILU Press Canada, 1997.
Washington, Salim. "Responses to Crossover Dreams." In *Race Traitor.* Noel Ignatiev and John Garvey, ed. New York: Routledge, 1996.
Weinfeld, Morton, and Lori A. Wilkinson. "Immigration, Diversity and Minority Communities." In *Race and Ethnic Relations in Canada.* Peter S. Li, ed. Second edition. Toronto: Oxford University Press, 1999.
Wildman, Stephanie M., and Adrienne Davis. "Making Systems of Privilege Visible." In *Critical Whiteness Studies: Looking Behind the Mirror.* Richard Delgado and Jean Stefancic, ed. Philadelphia: Temple University Press, 1997.
Woods, Ellen Meiksins. "Capitalism." *New Socialist* 37 (August-September, 2002).
————. *Empire of Capital.* London: Verso, 2003.